Micky—
Thanks for
spreading
the love

XO
Heidi

LOVE
LESSONS

104 Dates and the Stories
that Led Me to True Love

LOVE
LESSONS

104 Dates and the Stories that Led Me to True Love

HEIDI B. FRIEDMAN

Halo
PUBLISHING
INTERNATIONAL

Halo
PUBLISHING
INTERNATIONAL

Halo Publishing International
7550 W IH-10 #800, PMB 2069,
San Antonio, TX 78229

First Edition, February 2025
ISBN: 978-1-63765-726-3
Library of Congress Control Number: 2024924050

The information contained within this book is strictly for informational purposes. Unless otherwise indicated, all the names, characters, businesses, places, events and incidents in this book are either the product of the author's imagination or used in a fictitious manner. Any resemblance to actual persons, living or dead, or actual events is purely coincidental.

Halo Publishing International is a self-publishing company that publishes adult fiction and non-fiction, children's literature, self-help, spiritual, and faith-based books. We continually strive to help authors reach their publishing goals and provide many different services that help them do so. We do not publish books that are deemed to be politically, religiously, or socially disrespectful, or books that are sexually provocative, including erotica. Halo reserves the right to refuse publication of any manuscript if it is deemed not to be in line with our principles. Do you have a book idea you would like us to consider publishing? Please visit www.halopublishing.com for more information.

Contents

Introduction

THE JOURNEY TO LOVE

The greatest pleasure in life is love.
—**Euripides**

This book was written in two parts over fifteen years. While it may appear that I am just an extremely slow writer, I took a hiatus of over a decade. The first part of this book summarizes the research about love that I conducted when I was sad, lonely, and confused. This coincided with my fortieth birthday, a time when most of us stop to assess the reality of our life and figure out what is missing.

What was missing for me was real love. I mean the deep *Jerry Maguire* "you complete me" kind of love. I found myself baffled by the uncertainty around what it meant to be deeply in love and to find your soulmate. When I started writing over a decade ago, I titled the draft of the book *Embracing the Grey* because love was this elusive grey concept to me at a time when I saw life in black and white.

In an attempt to define this intangible concept, I gathered data about love from people in love. While I am not a scientist by any measure, I am a data geek who loves research projects. The analytical portion of my brain evolved to all-new levels in law school. Thus, I launched my informal "love" research project in 2010. I was convinced at that time that there had to be definitive feelings, ideas, or concepts that defined love, and if I just spoke to enough people and conducted enough research, I could figure it out.

These initial chapters came to life after I had been divorced for about seven years and was well on my way to going on what would eventually be 104 dates. I am guessing that 104 dates may sound shocking, desperate, and perhaps even impossible to you. Yet, for some reason, after the first few dates, I decided to start counting. Don't panic; I did not go out with 104 people. Over the nine and a half years between my divorce and finding the love of my life, I only went out with four people for any real length of time; they account for fifty-two of the dates. The guy I was dating when I wrote the initial chapters of this book won the prize with twenty-three dates over the course of six months.

So we are really talking about maybe fifty guys—does that sound more reasonable? I started a tally chart that I kept in a small journal in the top drawer of a dresser next to my bed, and after I met my true love, I burned it. It was quite gratifying.

There were many times during this dating marathon that I felt as if I were on an awful reality TV show, but I also had some of the funniest experiences of my entire life. Like laugh out loud, "I cannot believe this is happening to me" funny. There were plenty of rejections during this time as well. You know those guys who I was convinced were the perfect fit but had no interest in a short lawyer with two small kids. Can you believe it? There is no real way to convey in words what it is like to put yourself out there so many times while remaining so unsure of what you are looking for. I did not know how true love looked or felt.

My Cupid's quest did not come at the expense of embracing my independence and making sure that I was a strong female role model for my kids and others. I do not want any misunderstandings; I did not feel that I needed a man in my life to survive or even to thrive. I was then, and I am now, a strong-willed, self-built woman. I promised myself when I was young that I would never be in a position that required me to rely on a man for my livelihood, and I stuck to that promise throughout my time at The Ohio State University and Case Western Reserve Law School. While it took quite a few loans and more sleepless nights with Diet Doctor Pepper than I would like to remember, I was proud that I could support my children and myself fully and completely. In fact, I am a true Girl Power gal, and one of my favorite quotes is "Here's to strong women; may we know them; may we be them; may we raise them" (Ada Lovelace).

Perhaps the best way to reflect my point of view about strong women is to say that I am a die-hard, fully committed Ruth Bader Ginsburg (RBG) fan with a ton of swag to go along with my obsession with this small female Jewish jurist. She was always my hero, and I envied and admired her relationship with the love of her life, Marty Ginsburg. I knew that if I had to go back and chat with my twenty-five-year-old self, I would say to be very careful about the partner you pick for life. It is a choice that can make or break many things, including a career.

After my divorce, it seemed very difficult to find a Marty Ginsburg. I became very good at doing and being on my own, functioning with a very supportive village behind me, albeit one that was also fixing me up constantly. I learned how to shut the toilet valve off and details about the circuit box, and I embraced taking out the trash, scheduling the snowplow guy, and doing all the things that a husband might handle (recognizing how sexist that statement is, but also being honest). Once I found a great handyman, plumber, and electrician, I was really set. (Fun fact: Generally, Jewish guys cannot really fix things anyway!) Yet I felt that I had so much love to give in a way I had never been given an opportunity to do so; thus, I was off to the races in an attempt to make my life complete and find my person.

I recognize that during this quest, I had many privileges that allowed me the time and space for this journey, including a life-changing au pair. I was able to embrace my independence because the career I built allowed me to support two kids, our dog, and even pay alimony. I recognize others may not be as fortunate, but I hope some of these themes and lessons can still allow anyone looking for love to find their way to a happy and full heart.

Part II of the book is my own love story after I crossed the finish line and found my guy. I frankly forgot about part I until I found it on my computer almost fourteen years later, twelve years into a relationship with the love of my life, to whom I have been married for almost ten years. When I met Will, true love could not have been clearer to me. I credit my research and many, many bad dates with allowing me to have a much better understanding of love and for opening my heart to receive it. As I said to Will as part of my wedding vows, the path that led me to him, albeit very bumpy and winding, was one I would take all over again as long as I could in the end have him in my life as my husband and partner.

When I sat back and thought about all that I had learned throughout this lengthy and painful process, I developed the last part of the book to share my Love Lessons Learned (LLL) with the goal of helping others on their journey to find or maybe keep love. While I am not a fan of telling people what to do or how to do it, I am hoping that sharing what I learned through my research and dating marathon may save one or two people from making the same mistakes or may encourage them to take the chances I wish I would have taken. Overall, my main LLL is not to settle, which I will explain in great detail, but which also needs no real explanation at all. Oh, and of course, don't have too many rules or limits. Mine eroded over time, which opened up my path to love.

These love stories are here to provide others a foundation from which to launch their own journeys to happily ever after—whether it's for the first time or, as with me, the second time, which is most definitely the charm.

Part I
LOVE STORIES

Chapter 1

40 AND MISSING LOVE

Love is space and time measured by the heart.
—Marcel Proust

I woke up one morning shortly after my fortieth birthday and realized that I did not think I had ever been in love. At least with a living, breathing male human being. Of course, that does not include my youngest son who is certainly my favorite male on the planet and who very well may be, along with his older sibling, the ultimate love of my life. And that does not include all the things I have fallen in love with at one point or another. I certainly was in love with my Starbucks chai latte for years before I realized how much sugar was in it, and I definitely was in love with *Grey's Anatomy* for a while until it got to be too much like *ER* (too heavy on the gore, not enough drama). I still am in love with hot yoga, *Us Weekly*, and a really good pedicure. But let's be honest, people; those things can only make your heart flutter for so long.

I was not one of those people who never dated or walked down the aisle. In fact, I have had my fair share of boyfriends and was married for nine years. The closest I came to being truly in love before Will was my high school boyfriend, but I do not believe that you are capable of much more than puppy love at age sixteen. Sure, he was a great guy, and I lost more than my obsession with Jordache jeans when I was with him. But even after the Air Supply concerts and proms, I came to the conclusion that you have to be a fully developed "you" before you can be in love with someone else. Sure, there are a few couples whom I interviewed who are in love with their high school sweethearts, but maybe they just knew who they were much earlier than I did.

You may be wondering how I could have been married without ever having been in love. Let's call it more of a timing thing. After years of therapy and more copays than are countable, I have come to realize that, like every aspect of my life, I had a plan, and when I have a plan, I execute. My plan was to get married and have kids before I turned thirty, so when there was someone whom I connected with and the timing was right, I went for it. Yes, I settled, but I did love my husband, just not in the true-love, true-partner way I was looking for on my journey. I do not have a single regret about those years because I have two incredible children who bring me joy virtually every day.

Divorce changes a person though. It forces you to look inside and see what is missing. This is even worse when you are a serial overanalyzer. Divorce causes you to stop the train, get off earlier than you planned, and figure out what direction you are headed before you get back on so you do not continue to travel in the wrong direction. For me, it became a time of significant introspection, more so than at any other point in the almost four decades I had been on this earth up to that point. Once I figured out where I had come from, I spent time trying to decipher where I was going.

Eventually I decided to head in the direction of finding the "right" person. My person. But how was I going to get there? My initial plan was to start postdivorce dating—which, by the way, was more challenging than the divorce itself. Frankly, it made every legal motion I ever drafted or client meeting I ever prepared for look like a piece of cake.

Let's start with the initial challenge of trying to balance a full-time career as a partner in a law firm with raising two kids, spending time with your friends, and fitting in workouts. Suddenly, shaving your legs and finding something sexy but not too revealing to wear sounds like way too much work when the alternative is sitting on your bed, eating popcorn, and watching *The Bachelorette*. Nevertheless, my drive for finding the right guy had to start somewhere.

First, there were the fix-ups. When you are divorced and in your late thirties, everyone—and I mean everyone—fixes you up. There were so many times when, after only five minutes, I was trying desperately to figure out a speedy exit and wondering how my so-called friend thought this guy was going to be a match for me. That's when I was so thankful to have young kids and lots of excuses. Once I got past the initial fix-ups, I was ready for the big leagues, and it was time for the ever-popular Match.com (remember, this was 2010). Online dating may certainly be efficient, but it takes quite a bit of patience to weed out the shirtless photos and serial killers.

I quickly realized that finding love was going to be a marathon rather than a 5K, yet this glass-half-empty chick tried to remain optimistic. I fell in lust pretty early on in the online dating process. At the time, I thought it was love, but I later learned through my research that love is not so hard, not so hurtful, and not so complicated. I kept reading profiles and answering a few winks here and there, and eventually I met a wonderful guy. He did not look anything like the person I pictured myself with, but I figured a few drinks and a lot of laughs may be just what I needed. Yet as we continued to drink and laugh, I found myself struggling to figure out whether I was in love with him.

He was a divorced father reeling from a marriage that ended pretty badly, and he was having the same problem I was in trying to figure out what happily ever after looked like. After many discussions about the fact that neither of us really knew what constituted being in love, I started to believe that maybe there was more to the mystery of being in love than chalking it up to two bitter, divorced overanalyzers.

So I did what any normal forty-year-old, confused attorney would do—I went to see a psychic. Twenty dollars later, she assured me that I had a very happy, healthy future, which she predicted would include getting married and staying married, but she claimed she could not tell me if I was with the right guy and certainly could not tell me if I was in love. Instead, she told me I needed to figure that out for myself; of course, I could come back for a tarot-card reading for another forty dollars, and she could help me work through it.

Well, as tempting as tarot cards may be, I decided to start asking all the people around me how they knew they were in love with their spouse or significant other and how their person was "the one." How did they know it was love, and how had they stayed in love? After launching into my pursuit of love stories, I quickly determined that my current Match.com connection was not a match. We parted ways, and I continued on my quest to figure out the key to being in love and ideally staying in love.

Pursuing "the answer" is the way I tend to react to complex challenges. I need to figure out the reason for everything. At that time, love was foggy and unclear to me, and I was longing for it to be clear and identifiable. I had lived my entire life making things fit into clean, neat categories, often with actual labels on boxes, so I was determined to find a clean and clear path to love as well. I was convinced there had to be strategic themes for me to follow in order to know and feel true love. Like any good thesis, this proved to be true. I discovered that the individual love stories had various things in common, themes that I could embrace and understand.

I focused on interviewing people whom I knew fairly well and had a strong relationship with at the time so that I had a baseline understanding of who they were and what they were about. This foundation allowed me to analyze their answers a bit more deeply. While I contemplated randomly interviewing strangers, since I spent enough time in airports and at soccer games and dance recitals, I decided against it. The random approach did not seem logical to me when I was trying to piece together this puzzle; knowing the couple (or at least half of the couple) became as important as understanding their responses to my questions.

Most of the people I interviewed immediately told me when they knew they were in love—the specific moment or event. The couples explained it was when "she made me French toast for breakfast" or when "he put his hand on my shoulder when we crossed the street." There were stories of bar scenes and camping and college visits as the origins of the love stories. Not a single person used the cheesy yet popular "it was love at first sight." While a few people described seeing their future spouse across a crowded room and thinking "she is cute" or "he is handsome," the love part seemed to come a bit later and usually in an expected way, at least in my subset of lovebirds.

Listening to these blasts from the past was fun, but I really wanted to understand what it was about the other person that made them know that it was the right person and that they were truly in love. Plus, how did they know it was not just lust or attraction or even the right timing but not the right person? I needed to know more about the feeling than the event.

I have an uncanny ability to have insights into the relationships of my friends. I may have missed my calling as a therapist, although psychology definitely plays a role in the practice of law. It is hard to believe that I could be so bad at figuring out my own personal life, but yet so good at seeing deeply into the lives of those around me. I am able to see what makes people fit together. For example, I fixed up one of my now closest friends with her husband who was my BFF from law school, and they are happily married with three kids. These insights allowed me to pick the pool for my research by focusing on people who seemed both happy and confident in their choice of partner.

In order to have a diverse set of data, it was important to hear a diverse set of love stories. Those who were newly married as well as those married for forty-plus years. Those who were just dating and those who were married but had lost their spouses. Those in same-sex relationships and those who had chosen a spouse a bit older, younger, or from a different background. I spoke to several people who were on their second marriage, which I would come to learn is often viewed a bit differently than the first.

Most of the people I interviewed never really stopped to think about how they knew their partner was the one. Instead, they just "knew" it was love and moved ahead. While the love stories varied, virtually all of them were emblematic of what I was searching so hard to find. Some of these conversations brought out my jealous side on occasion, as my blind acceptance of my previous relationships did not fall into this category—I never really knew whether I was in love with any of these people or not. Attempting to figure out how the person knew that the relationship was actually love seemed to be the key to the mystery.

The easiest interviews were with the few newlyweds. Hell, I cannot remember what I did yesterday, so it makes sense that the closer in time to falling in love you are, the easier it is to remember the answer to how you knew it was love. It is also easier to retrieve this information prior to when your life is taken over by carpools, homework, and figuring out who is going to the grocery store or picking up the birthday treat. It became clear as well that love evolves over time. The reason you love somebody two kids, one sickness, and three job losses later can be very different than the reason you initially fell in love with that person.

While most of my conversations led me to answers, there were a few times that my perception did not align with reality or with the person I was interviewing and their evaluation of their own love story or whether they were really in love. Sometimes the person we think is the right person can turn out not to be, and we grow in different directions. Life is not predictable, so is it even possible to predict whether you picked the right person to go through it with you? Sometimes you are too young when you make your pick, or maybe you have not worked through your problems. Or, like me, maybe you rushed your pick a bit to get to another goal.

All these things may lead us to ask for a do-over. It was this do-over that I wanted to get right. It was this do-over that drove my quest to understand why one person makes the right choice and picks their true partner for life, while another chooses the wrong person.

Even after hearing all these love stories, I was not able to find a simple single answer to my questions. Yet the more people I interviewed, the more I started hearing different versions of the same answers. It became easy to sort these answers into a few categories. Eventually, the themes presented themselves. These themes appeared to be questions to ask yourself when you are contemplating whether to dive in deeper or run for the hills. I was confident that I had unlocked several significant insights into the elusive feeling of love. These conversations revealed definitive principles that appear to lead to magnificent love affairs, families, and happiness. So let's start by diving into the love stories!

Chapter 2

THE BEST YOU

At the touch of love, everyone becomes a poet.
—**Plato**

In digging into these love stories, the loudest and clearest theme I heard was that being with their "person" brought out the best in them. "He made me a better person," reported a forty-year-old stay-at-home mom married for eleven years. "She brought out the best in me," said a lawyer friend who had been happily married for nine years. The widow remembering her husband of almost fifty years answered that "he definitely made me the best person I could be." This response turned out to be my personal favorite.

I knew the opposite of the best. I was in a relationship (using the term *relationship* very loosely) that brought out the worst in me, and it was not my marriage. It was a post-divorce fling that made me needy and insecure. In its short life, there was more drama than is typical during an entire lifetime, but it helped my overall growth to see what does not work for me. After a few dates, I learned that the guy I was seeing had a problem with alcohol. I found myself moving toward my tendency as a fixer (think *Scandal*'s Olivia Pope), a classic tendency that I had relied on many times before in relationships. This was not me at my best. Rather, it was a historical default that had led me down some unhealthy roads, but at least I was smart enough this time to see it, call it, and end it quickly.

I think deep down we all want to be the best version of ourselves. Living our life as our best self provides us validation and self-esteem, but being your best self is not easy. It takes a lot of work to reach your true potential, but "nothing worth having comes easy" (Theodore Roosevelt). Becoming your best self takes practice, it takes knowing what "best" looks like; it takes self-awareness and the ability to understand your own strengths and weaknesses as well as your potential. That is why I was so moved by the love stories that included a partner helping someone achieve this goal.

The concept of "best self" made me think of Malcom Gladwell's book *Outliers*. In it, Gladwell shares the premise that individuals who are successful and have reached their true potential have gotten to that point because they practiced more often and put in more effort, but they also had luck on their side. This made me think that if dating is considered practice, I was pretty convinced, according to Gladwell's model, I would be reaching my true potential very soon. Yet luck was not a concept I could embrace since it did not seem to like me much. I literally have never won anything except an occasional game of Rummy Cube. Send me to Vegas, and I will lose your money. These musings, however, made me wonder if people could make their own luck.

I carried around *The Secret* at one point during my early dating days. I read it on flights and before bed in an effort to convince myself that I could manifest the love for which I was looking so hard. The book was "a thing" at that time. The premise of the book was much less complex than that of *Outliers* since it only required you to visually and physically live the life you wanted to have in order to make it happen. No real practice required. Just pure manifestation. My commitment to that process quickly died along with my hope that I was ever going to be lucky enough to find "the one."

This may be a good place to pose the question of fate and whether there is really a soulmate for everyone. I want to believe in fate. Fay, the psychic, is probably cursing me for even questioning it, but I do not believe there is just one soulmate for everyone, especially not after hearing all these wonderful people explain how and why they were in love with their partners. Match.com would be out of business if everyone had just one soulmate. What if mine is somewhere in Tanzania, or if he gave up on me already and is married to his non-soulmate, living in a great house in Nebraska?

There is a Jewish word for soulmate—*bashert*. The short definition is "destined" or "meant to be." My parents are absolutely bashert, and oftentimes I hear stories that include crazy, random occurrences that lead to true love, so bashert has to be a thing. My philosophy, for what it is worth, is that there are at least several people out there who will be true partners at different points of your life. It is more of a matter of timing and connection than anything else. It is shared principles, values, and viewpoints about life and the future that make someone one of your soulmates.

Unfortunately, though, they do not sell soulmates at Nordstrom. Instead, the closest thing there is to a soulmate store is Eharmony, Jdate, and, of course, Match. The online dating shops are at least one way to see if there is a soul out there that connects with yours. At some point, you may be faced with the situation of whether that connection could mean more, whether that connection allows you to feel your best, be your best, and, of course, be in love. This is what I was trying to figure out—how do you know?

As I dug further through the various responses I received from people who discussed becoming their best through their relationships, I realized that someone's best is extremely subjective and specific. Sure, if you have a person who is not a good communicator, and he gets into a relationship with someone who gives him the space and support to share his feelings, then that may allow him to have a better, stronger relationship. I purposefully said "him" here because I know very few women who have trouble communicating. Or your best may be that your love may know just how to defuse you if you are a freak-out overreactor type. Maybe your best is that you can actually just be yourself, but a calmer, happier version.

Then there is next-level best. This is when someone can elevate themselves by sharing their life with another person who inspires them to go the extra mile or take on the next challenge. As cliché as this may sound, some of the most successful duos I spoke with credit their partners for the support and inspiration to do better and be better. These explanations usually came up when the subject was discussing his or her career. One person even talked specifically about having the courage to start her own business, which was her dream, because her spouse took a job that would allow them to have the stability they would need for her to live that dream. One of my favorite discussions was when one of the women I spoke to explained that she would not be in the C-suite at the company she was working for if it were not for her husband pushing her, supporting her, and agreeing to bear much more of the kid burden to make space for her success. She felt as if he saw so much more potential in her than she saw in herself. She seemed to have found her own Marty Ginsburg—what a dream!

I personally struggled with what my best self even looked like. I knew it was not the person I was at the end of my marriage when guilt pervaded my every thought. Two years after my divorce, I was still trying to manage that guilt. My journal at that that time reminds me of the intensity of those negative feelings:

> *I have spent so much of my time trying to ease my guilt for making what I know in my heart and soul is the right choice for me. I think part of the hole I have is the part of me that I feel I gave up. I hope that the missing piece is not gone forever, and I pray that I can fill it back up. I just*

don't know where to start. Maybe my guilt has
made this hole, and it will never close.

Lots of therapy helped me to work through what weighed me down and to continue on my journey toward becoming a stronger, more complete, more positive person. Yet I felt there was still plenty of work to be done in order to become my best self.

I noticed another thread throughout all the love stories—in order to feel as if you are at your best, you need to feel supported, loved, and very comfortable with your partner. So it may not just be that you are your best self, however you define it, but that there are other components associated with a true loving relationship that provide the foundation and support for you to find success in your relationship and your life.

I was starting to figure out that there are so many aspects to happy couples and what makes them work. I decided to reread *Outliers* and try to envision what my best self might look like as I continued to gather more love stories.

Chapter 3

THE BALANCE OF US

Being deeply loved by someone gives you strength, while loving someone deeply gives you courage.
—Lao Tzu

"I knew she had my back," expressed a thirty-three-year-old personal trainer married for ten years. A fifty-five-year-old restaurant owner married for over twenty-five years explained, "I just knew he would take care of me." She still gets butterflies in her stomach when he walks into the room.

This theme may speak more to the longevity of relationships than any other theme. Feeling supported came up most often in my conversations with people who had been married for some length of time. There is no better example of this than my own parents. I asked my mom the "how did you know you were in love" question, and her response was that she knew my dad would take care of her, and she felt safe with him and fully supported. At the time I asked the question, they had been together for forty-seven years, married for forty-three. They are each other's best friend. They complete each other's sentences and laugh at each other's jokes. They still love being together and value their time away together almost as much as their time with their grandchildren. They protect each other and care for each other. When my dad is in pain, my mom is in pain. When my mom needs anything, my dad will drop everything to help her, support her, and comfort her. They are a well-oiled machine.

Their ability to support each other has been tested. It was tested throughout the Vietnam War, many surgeries, quite a few job losses, too many financial crises to count, raising and caring for their children, and losing both their parents. They give new meaning to surviving hard times, and they don't always take it in stride. But what they do is hold each other's hands and take turns supporting each other when the other person needs it. How in the world my mother knew that feeling at age seventeen when my dad put his hand on her back and they crossed the street is mind-boggling to me. Sure, those were simpler times with fewer distractions, but none of the things that cut into a couple's ability to support each other has shaken them. Clearly, I did not inherit the gene of being able to figure love out so quickly and easily.

I have spent many therapy sessions and countless hours trying to figure out why someone with parents who have such a strong marriage has had so many unsuccessful and wrong relationships. And it's not just me. Neither of my two sisters has been married. One sister had a few close calls and even a broken engagement, but both are very much single. The only two grandchildren in the family belong to me. Lucky for them, they are the sole targets of my parents' spoiling, gifts, and grandparent shenanigans. I am very different from my sisters on many levels, so evaluating them and why they were not "in love" did not provide much insight for me.

In trying to figure out what it was about me that did not correlate to my parents, I wondered if my independent self would be open to the level of support I had seen my parents provide to each other. I knew I needed someone in my life whom I could rely on, but could I let someone take care of me? I think my picture is next to the definition of *caretaker* in Webster's dictionary. I have taken care of everyone and everything in my life. In fact, I now realize that in addition to my inappropriate focus on fixing people, I also subconsciously sought significant others who needed to be take care of, which is one of the reasons why I ended up in these uneven relationships. I even have data to back that up. When I took the Enneagram test through the Enneagram Institute, my type is a 2, the Helper, and I am a strong 2. That was followed by the Loyalist (a type 6), a positive quality in the scheme of things, and one I hoped would help me on my relationship quest.

When thinking back to why I picked people whom I could help, I think I seemed to get a rush from helping others manage their issues—that's so much easier than dealing with my own problems, I guess. I tended to date the underdog, the guy who needed some extra support (emphasis on *extra*). I tend to do this outside of romantic relationships as well. If there is a problem, I like to solve it. I am the one who believes you always show up and go the extra mile, and I can truly say that I don't look for anything in return. But as I contemplated what a true partnership would look like, which is what I was hoping to achieve, I spent quite a bit of time trying to figure out if I could make space for someone to help me? Maybe there was another type 2 out there somewhere, and he was handsome and single and lived in Cleveland.

I clearly remember sitting in the office of the couples' therapist at the end of my marriage and discussing this very issue. This therapist was "the" marriage guru, and he had just told my ex-husband and me that there was nothing left to save in our relationship. The therapist's announcement that it was time to move on was no surprise to me. I already knew this fact, but I am a big fan of third-party validation, especially when you are about to break up a family and know that the lives of your six-year-old and three-year-old would never be the same. I confessed to the therapist that I was exhausted, and for once in my life, I wanted someone to take care of me.

"Do you think you would ever be able to do that, because I am not sure you would," he advised me. Wow. Was I so controlling that I could not pass the baton to allow someone else to run the next leg of the race?

I might not have been able to let someone take care of me then, but I know that I can now. Don't be fooled into thinking I am ready to give up all decision-making and let someone else make all plans, pay all the bills, and decide what car we will buy or where to send the kids to camp.

I have become much better at letting go of some things, even if it's just picking out the cake to make for the cake walk (or the brownies to buy at Whole Foods and pretend you made them for the cake walk), buying birthday presents, or picking out clothes for the kids. Despite maintaining some control over the little things, I have realized how much happier I am and how much easier life is with someone to share the burden of making the decisions that really count—the ideal situation, taking care of each other.

A therapist I used to see (and yes, I am a big fan of therapy, if you have not noticed), when I was in the miserable struggle of deciding whether to end my marriage, explained to me that marriage is really similar to being in an ocean. Every couple will have waves in their lives. Some will be big waves, and some will be small waves, but those waves keep coming. Sometimes when you are barely standing up after being hit by the last wave, an even bigger wave will knock you right back over. The key to success in this ocean of life is taking turns pulling each other up. If one person is always doing the pulling up, it will not work. That is not a partnership, and that is a dynamic that is destined to fail. As a recovering "puller upper," I related to this story like no other. Maybe it was because I am scared to be in the ocean. I am so not a great swimmer, although I do love looking at the water. Or maybe because I actually pictured myself standing in the water and falling over again and again, having to push myself up and pull others with me. I woke up at night out of breath and out of hope.

All these happily married people I interviewed found love in the ability to lean on someone else. I always picture that ridiculous team-building exercise where you are supposed to close your eyes and fall backwards into someone's arms and trust that they will catch you. I am not the most trusting person in the first place, and letting go is not generally my strong suit, but the concept has always intrigued me.

My goal in life has been to find a true equal partner. Not in the typical sense. As a lawyer in a big firm, I have over 200 partners already, I always knew I needed a life partner. Someone who was able to share the burdens, discuss life decisions, and help find solutions. To share the so-called profits, but also the losses. Someone I knew I could count on because there is no doubt in my mind that I was in a position to be able to hold up my end of the partnership.

What was so interesting is that some find the concept of partnership cold and professional. I, however, was not using the term *partner* in a cold, formulaic way. I always figured that if I was truly in love, that person would be my partner in every aspect of my world; it would be a partnership like Mike and Carol Brady's. Others may see me as a lawyer trying to push my profession into my personal life. I will admit that I often view life as a lawyer, but I was not backing down on the partnership concept that I was convinced made relationships work. What I know after hearing so many love stories is that the relationships that work well have a foundation that is based on this very kind of partnership. They are the people who feel that they have a significant other in their life who will never let them down, and this allows them to open their hearts and their lives to love.

One couple my age explained that they tag-teamed on the hard issues. He explained that his aging parents were causing a ton of stress that he was trying to manage, while their young kids were having friend issues and school changes that his wife took control of for the most part. It was a true divide and conquer that worked from the get-go as life got complex after that Hawaiian honeymoon as family, kids, and work threw things their way on a daily basis.

Another older woman, my adopted nana, recounted stories of sicknesses when her now-deceased husband would take incredibly good care of her, and then what she went through when he became so sick that she cared for him for years until he passed away. These were life's biggest waves that could really pull you down, but she explained that their support for each other was balanced, and they took turns giving and receiving. "We took care of each other, and our love got us through the hardest of times. I miss him every single day," she recounted.

Nana explained that one person cannot be solely responsible for the happiness and strength of the whole family. Sure, there are times when she felt she needed to take on that role, but she and her husband passed that weight back and forth many times. Nana experienced one of the worst losses a person can experience when her grandson was killed in a car accident. The first thing she wished for during that time was that her dear husband were still alive to pull her up from the feeling that she was drowning in an ocean of grief. She missed the strength and support of the love of her life when the biggest waves hit her. But she is tough, and she was able to pull herself and so many around her up from many tragedies. She really was an example of an independent woman making space for the right man to enhance her life and help her ride the waves.

I cried during this conversation in an empathetic way, but also out of true sadness that I could not shake the wonder of whether I was going to eventually get old and sick and have to count on my children to take care of me. At that moment, the vision was hard to picture since we were still at the point that my kids could not take care of themselves. Rather than going down that rabbit hole, I decided to focus on Nana's wisdom in describing balance, a concept I appreciated due to my love of yoga. My yoga practice always tells me when I am the most balanced, as my headstands and crows don't work if life on or off my mat is not working.

So I tried to visualize the perfect headstand, and a calm came over me. I tried to digest what supporting one another in a relationship might look like and how it might feel. The good news is that looking at the ocean is my happy place, so picturing someone holding my hand in the water and making sure I did not drown was an inspirational image for me as I continued on my journey to find love.

Chapter 4

EFFORTLESSLY AT HOME

Two souls with but a single thought,
two hearts that beat as one.
—**John Keats**

As I dove into these conversations about love, I continued to find themes in the responses. "I felt totally comfortable with him, as if I had known him forever. I felt like I was home," added a thirty-seven-year-old COO who had been married to her husband for about a year. She was a good case study for me because she was one of the ones who had held out. Working through her fair share of boyfriends, with whom there was always something missing, she stood her ground and eventually found the guy with whom she was able to be herself and who embraced her "crazy," as she kindly referred to it. In fact, she reached out and grabbed my hands over the table during our lunch when she was answering my many questions, as I think she saw the tears that welled up in my eyes as I looked at her, in awe of her patience; my vibe must of just exuded the sadness and loneliness I felt at that time. We both agreed that we all have our own crazy, and she explained that her now husband actually thinks her crazy is cute. Yes, it may have been new love at that time, but when I see them together now, they still fit.

A friend married for twelve years provided a similar response: "I could finally be me—100-percent myself." They have one of the best marriages I have been able to personally witness. She has a leg up. Her mom was a marriage counselor who in her day shared her incredible wisdom on shows like *Phil Donahue*. Her mom's golden rules of keeping your marriage happy once you find the right person are so basic. It requires a recipe of one night together, alone, each week, one weekend away together each month, and one week away together each year. Puerto Rico or Europe may not be in the cards every year, but there is something about stopping the world and reconnecting back to what brought you together in the first place that rings true to me. I found that taking time for reconnection sans kids seemed to be a major key as I interviewed my "in love" targets about how they are able to keep their love alive. But at the time, finding the guy to sip piña coladas with on the beach in Cabo was a challenge.

Then there were the high school sweethearts. The couple who had been married for fifteen years and still considered themselves best friends. She also described feeling completely at ease, comfortable, and connected to her spouse from the start, which allowed her to know she was "in love." This is the guy who calls the restaurant for her girl's-night fortieth birthday bash to send wine over to the table and includes an iced tea for his bride because she does not drink for medical reasons. Thoughtful and caring is an understatement. I proceeded to drink her share of the wine, as I concluded that this was a guy who understood her as I witnessed firsthand her feeling of comfort and support from him.

Nana also shared that for her, it was the simple fact that "he made me feel special." Even though her husband has been gone for well over ten years, she can recreate that feeling of comfort and ease just by talking about him. This was not her first marriage either, although she will tell you she had wanted to marry her true love in the first place, as she knew him before she married her first husband. Here is where that crazy concept of timing comes into play, but she explained that "when it is *right*, you just know"—seven words that at the time, I could not get my head around and that caused me quite a bit of turmoil. If I had been able to understand what that meant, I would not have needed to set out on my quest.

Plus, it "feels right" was way too unclear for me back then—I was hoping for flashing red hearts or something a bit more tangible. What about those of us who won't let ourselves know love because we are scared? Would there be no hesitation if it was right? I found that hard to believe at my age, as I was considering whether I wanted to merge my already-overcomplicated life with two kids with another person who had his own complications and, more likely than not, his own kids. It couldn't be as easy as just feeling it is right. Call me a cynic or call me a realist—I just was not buying this "it feels right" concept.

I found another entry in my journal from this time that reminded me of how I struggled with identifying this so-called feeling:

> *So what does the right relationship look like? Can I be happy? Why do I always look for what is wrong and expect so much? I wish I had answers to these questions.*

My journal entry goes on to analyze the guy whom I was dating at the time, as we were about ten dates in at that point. I decided that I would know when it was right and that my quest to find the right person was becoming clearer. I was in fact searching for some type of feeling that I was starting to articulate:

> *Find the person that makes nothing else matter.*

This seemed to be the best explanation of my goal. So I continued to pursue answers.

One older man smiled in response to my "how did you know" question and said, "She fit like an old sock." I laughed at this one because I never kept socks or any type of clothes too long, as I am a "donate it if you have not worn it in the past two years" person. He went on to explain that he has a favorite pair of socks that he has had forever; they are soft and cozy and have basically molded to his feet in a good way. In a way that allows him to feel so comfortable on a freezing Cleveland winter day. He said that his bride was just like that sock, so comfortable at first, but now molded to him. Being with her makes him feel warm and cozy and at home. Tell me you cannot picture this sweet man with his comfy socks and beautiful wife cuddled together by the fire. Talk about goals!

Yet there were several other subjects that explained that he or she "just got me" feeling. Having someone understand you is exhilarating. My closest friends get me, but I am not sure my parents even get me. Maybe I am harder to get? Maybe I have too many walls up that need to be broken down before the real me can be gotten? Thinking alike certainly helps, and that came through loud and clear in the interviews. When you view life through the same lens, even if you approach it a little bit differently, it is easier to connect in a way that feels as if you are understood on every level. Many of the love stories included confirmation that the couple shared many of the same life visions, and a few even joked about how they sometimes have the exact same thoughts. I jotted down the world *magical* next to that concept in my notebook.

This general ease of being with your significant other intrigued me. Sometimes I did not have the opportunity to interview the other half of the couple, which often left me with only half of the story. My guess is that their partner would also feel "gotten" because these love stories confirmed that understanding each other was the foundation for a successful relationship. There was the explanation I heard several times from different people who relied on the ease of the relationship as the explanation as to how they knew it was right. "I just felt like I was home."

Well, every home needs a foundation. My take is that sometimes you have to live in a house or two (or ten) to find the one that you really want. The house analogy to these love stories may be a bit simplistic, but our home is the one place where we can let go and be comfortable. How often do you hear the expression that someone wants to make you feel "at home." Although my personal favorite is "Home is where the heart is."

I will tell you where home is not. Home is not with a guy you agree to meet at a bar after connecting on Match. com and, five minutes into the conversation, he asks your legal advice related to a cease-and-desist order he received from Pepsi associated with some random business he runs out of his garage. No, instead, this drives you to return to your actual home as fast as possible. This is one of the times that I was so grateful that I could use my kids as an excuse to leave, and when I say leave, I mean run for the car. Plus, this guy did not even remotely look like his picture on Match, which was likely over a decade old, just to make the whole experience more of a fail.

So why has it been so hard for me to find that connection, that person who gets me completely and whom I could be 100-percent myself with at all times? I realized that I seemed to be holding back. I have always been afraid to share the real me and all my "crazy," but I have realized through this process that the crazy has to come out because we all have crazy. This includes my tendency to overcommunicate and my ridiculous obsession with overthinking every...damn...thing, from what shoes I will wear to whether the guy I am with really likes me.

The key that makes or breaks whether you can truly be in love with a person is how he or she responds to your crazy. Someone who embraces your crazy is probably a keeper, but you have to want to embrace his crazy as well. Once you find that, though, apparently it just fits and feels right, like the perfect house or that old sock.

Chapter 5

CLASHING BUT CONNECTED

Love is a condition in which the happiness
of another person is essential to your own.
—**Robert A. Heinlein**

The love stories included more than just cupcakes and roses. Many of the lovebirds I interviewed admitted that they fought on occasion, some more often than others. I usually had to push a bit to ask if they ever disagreed, but then I heard explanations of how well they fought and then made up as proof of how good they were together.

It is only logical that two humans living under the same roof, many with kids, would occasionally get angry, or at least miffed, and fight. Plus, it is pretty much a universal concept that life is not easy, and when we are stressed, our fuses are short, and we take things out on those who are closest to us. A close family friend in her midfifties noted, "When you are really in love, you may feel as if you hate the person more than anything at that specific moment, but you still do not want them to leave."

It is rather amazing how closely connected love and hate are; at first glance, they seem to be polar-opposite concepts. Both love and hate require the same level of emotion. If strong emotions are involved, you can love very deeply and hate with equal intensity. It just depends on whether your emotions make you feel very good or very bad. I always tell my kids, though, that hate is a very strong word and to be careful how they use it. Come on, do you really hate brussels sprouts or brushing your teeth (maybe the former, but definitely not the latter)? I felt as if *hate* was a little dramatic and even improper when describing the challenges involved in these love stories. In fact, most of the interviewees explained that they wanted their spouse close to them even during a fight, and they never felt hatred toward their partner, even at the worst of times. Rather, it usually was the passion that drove the disappointment or the temporary ill will, and at the end of the fight, it was the deep love and connection that sustained the relationship.

Apparently, a fight can also provide confirmation that someone is your "forever" love. A twenty-three-year-old student, then married for just a few months, retold the story of how she knew she was "in love" and this guy was "it" when they got into a fight "over major issues." She recalled being incredibly angry, but she still could not imagine her life without him and did not want him to leave her. Not only did he not leave her, there were also flowers, ice cream (her favorite), and lots of "I'm sorrys" involved. Since this student spent a lot of her life with my family, I had the joy of seeing them together firsthand as a couple that truly fits together. In my speech at their wedding, I celebrated their love during a toast: "It is so important for you both to hear each other and see each other. You may not always agree, but you must always respect each other. You fit together so well, and I am honored to have been a witness to your love story."

Additionally, one of the major comments that came up repeatedly was the importance of not holding back your views or your feelings. Trapping or suppressing those does not serve you or anyone around you well. Instead, those feelings and views just gather steam and fire and then surface at inopportune times. It was a common response that any attempt to repress or hold back was actually an effort to not hurt the one who was loved. One husband whom I considered a dear friend explained that he learned to "keep my mouth shut" and live by the principle "Happy wife, happy life." Yet when I pushed and dug deeper, he explained that when he had a runway on which to share his concerns or annoyances, he felt heard and closer to his spouse. Holding back does not benefit anyone in the long run. Plus, no one is saying that sharing feelings always leads to a fight. In fact, not sharing them seems to lead to the big blowups.

Several of the love stories hyped up their ability to communicate and resolve issues, and a few of the couples I talked with reported that they hardly fought at all.

Instead, they may have needed a bit of space on occasion, but quickly and repeatedly expressed a fear that they could never lose their significant other. "I could never imagine my life without her, nor do I want to" was the honest reflection of a friend who had also just turned forty. "I have never been mad enough at him to even make him sleep on the sofa. I need him to be in our bed every single night," explained a workout buddy from the gym who had been married for almost thirty years. Her explanation reminded me of something my grandma Lilly told me years ago, which was, "You should never go to bed mad." She explained that she always kissed Grandpa Nate good night every night, and they let their troubles dissipate with that kiss.

Let's be real though. There is no possibility of having a relationship that does not include disagreements. If there are no fights, then one of the parties is not truly sharing their feelings or points of view. What I heard is that the key to these love stories is how you fight. In the strongest of relationships, the fighting is even constructive. These couples do not vomit up the five million things their wife may have done wrong over the past fifteen years, nor is there any hitting below the belt, even if it might make you feel better at that moment. Instead, one of my role-model couples explained to me that they fight in a way that allows them to be respectful of each other's views and focus on the issues before them and how to resolve them. Sure, there may be a storming out of the house and some bad words thrown around, but they are human. It is the coming back together after the process and working through to the solution, even if it is that they need to agree to disagree and move on, that is important.

In further discussing resolution, several couples explained that one of the main tools they use to diffuse a disagreement is to hug the other person. It may not be well received at first, but apparently it virtually always works. The first time I heard this during the interviews, I thought it was brilliant and filed it away as a best practice for future use. As I continued my research, several others talked about using the same "just go hug her" approach, explaining that feeling the physical connection with his spouse just made whatever they were fighting about dissipate. It's really hard to be angry when someone is hugging you, especially tightly.

I also discovered the concept of the feedback loop during my research; that is when one person in the relationship is having a hard time, and the close level of connection between the couple results in that anxiety or anger playing off each other, which elevates it. A feedback loop in a romantic relationship seems to be representative of the interconnectedness of some of these couples whose moods, albeit good or bad, also become intertwined. So these exceptional couples, who are so connected and feel at home with each other, also feel comfortable sharing their hardships. Recognizing the loop and cutting it off can be a challenge at times. Yet even anger does not eradicate love and appreciation when you are with the right partner, and many of the love stories included explanations that recognizing the loop and communicating about the challenge will right the wrong just about every time.

Overall, the love stories included explanations that there was nothing in this world any of my love gurus would allow to come between them or the family they had built. I appreciated such a positive spin on fighting with those you love, as I had witnessed some fairly bad, emotional fights in my day, ones that did not end the way these people explained. Postdivorce, I never turned down a request from a friend to meet with someone going through what I had already experienced. These meetings over lattes always took place when the woman getting the divorce was at the very bottom of the virtual hill she would need to climb to take her life back. At the point that she could not remotely envision the lovely walk down the postdivorce hill toward a path of independence. I have heard some scary, awful stories over coffee, tales that put my own life and challenges in perspective. People stay and tolerate abuse (verbal and even physical) for a variety of reasons—the main reason I heard over and over again was because they had one kid or several. I did my best to reserve judgment during these conversations, but mental and physical safety is nonnegotiable. Plus, there is plenty of data that confirms that modeling a healthy relationship for your kids is the greatest gift you can give them. I am grateful for that gift from my parents, and I hoped then to provide my kids with the same model someday. The healthy relationship can include ups and downs and disagreements, but productive, loving resolutions are the goal.

The other concept that came up when discussing disagreements was trust, as it appeared to be the glue that bound these couples together. Many of the couples talked about their trust in their significant other as the foundation for their marriage and something they always came back to if there was a disagreement. In contrast, when I was chatting with the women in the process of moving on from a marriage, time and time again, there were stories about lying, dishonesty, and erosion of trust. I experienced that myself in several relationships, and I believe some of those wounds have not yet scabbed. Trust is probably the most important thing to me in any relationship, and I think I missed my calling as a private investigator. I have spent way too much time trying to figure out if someone is being honest, or suspecting and searching to confirm a lie. I was hoping my truth antenna could eventually go down, and I could begin to feel more like these couples who trust each other enough to share their honest feelings, maybe even fight about what those feelings means and come back together in a way that makes them both feel heard and supported.

I decided that I could get behind having a responsible, constructive dispute with my significant other, especially if it ends with a hug. I have learned from this process that even the most wonderful love stories come with different viewpoints and certain times when one person may disappoint the other or make their person angry. I am not afraid of a good fight. I am an attorney, after all, who loves negotiation and, yes, winning. Yet, in love, it seems that you win some, and you lose some, but when you are with the right person, you always win.

Chapter 6

SIMPLY RIGHT

*One word frees us of all the weight
and pain in life. That word is love.*
—**Sophocles**

At first glance, the response I received over and over again about the origin of these love stories—"it was just so easy"—seemed to be repetitive of the "we just fit together" theme in chapter 4. Yet as I heard more and more love stories, the answers relating to ease were different because my interview subjects did not talk as much about feeling comfortable at home, but instead shared the way the couple could talk to each other or laugh together with ease, usually from the day they met. Thus, ease presented itself as a separate and important theme. There were no stories of rationalizing about any changes needed to be made for this relationship to work—no thoughts that "she will change that habit" or "I am sure he really wants to be more successful." Instead, the initial connection was like the last puzzle piece just fitting easily into the overall puzzle. I love puzzling—don't judge me!

My nana explained that with her second husband, who was the love of her life, the conversation came incredibly easily, and "we liked the same things—music, theater, and food." A friend my age announced that by the third date, she could show up in sweats and no makeup for a chill night, rather than spending time getting up before the alarm to put makeup on before her boyfriend woke up. I know someone who actually did this! Even when talking to those who were in my dream situation and giving things a go the second time around, their responses centered on the ease they felt with each other almost immediately. While it may have taken more of an effort initially to connect than if you were single without kids from another relationship, when they were together, it was as if they had been together all along.

In a desperate effort to understand this amazing concept of ease a bit more, I asked people to describe why it was so easy, other than just the conversation or laughter, when they found the love of their life. This was a question that was hard for many to answer with any real substance. "It was just so easy; that is all I can say," reiterated a neighbor when I pushed for a clearer answer. "It was as much a feeling as it was an experience—just calm and peaceful," explained one of my besties who was elated with her do-over that I helped initiate.

A newly married subject described the feeling as equivalent to sitting on a beach, listening to the waves and watching a sunset. This one shook me a bit since that is one of my very favorite experiences. I closed my eyes when I got home that night and pictured myself on a beach, listening to waves and watching the sunset, trying to envision who was sitting next to me as I drifted off to sleep. I ended up having a dream that night that I was buried in a sandcastle and could not get out. Clearly, the concept of ease was elusive to me.

Very little in my life has been easy. I can provide a long list of all the things I probably had to work a bit harder for than most, including having my kids. My first was born eight weeks early, at thirty-two weeks, for no apparent reason and weighed barely three pounds, and then I spent three months on bed rest with my second, most of it having to lie flat with an IV in my leg and a three-year-old in tow. The good news is that despite this lack of ease, things did work out. So my focus stayed on the concept that all is well that ends well, rather than on the ease of the process.

While I love a good challenge, the lure of bringing ease into my life sounded dreamy. It also felt very pie in the sky. A journal entry I scribbled after going to my therapist a few years ago highlights the challenge I faced at that time. I often asked her, "What does the right relationship look like?"

Her answer on this day was "Just like with Zach—just easy, calm, unconditional love."

This spoke to me, and I spent many weeks thinking about unconditional love and realizing that my relationships to date had way too many conditions. Maybe I was influenced by the launching of my interview process at that time, but I continued to explain to myself in my journal that:

> I want that unconditional love. I want to know when I wake up and when I go to sleep that the guy lying next to me really and truly loves me. I need a rock and a partner in life. Someone to make joint decisions with and someone to lean on. But I also need someone to laugh with me and have fun.

Clearly, the concept of ease had been planted in my head already, so it was fulfilling to see it play out as part of my research project.

The opposite of ease is trying to make a round peg fit into a square hole or, even worse, settling for something that does not fit at all or trying to hammer it in so that neither the peg nor the hole are recognizable. I had done this too many times. A few of the interviewees ended up identifying similar struggles, despite my perception that they were in love and happy. The common theme among these struggling couples was that one person was trying to change something about the other person, perhaps just as I had thought, "If he loves me, he will change." True change has to come from within and must be for yourself, not for someone else. Let's be clear, though; for the most part, by age forty, change is hard.

In fact, some days I wondered if I would ever be able to fit someone into the life I built, especially with the ease that I heard in these love stories. At a certain point, you get good at being alone and maybe a bit set in your ways. I am pretty sure eating popcorn in bed and watching *Sex in the City* is not the dream of most guys, at least the straight ones. Travel soccer games and weekend dance recitals? Oh, I am sure those events are on the top of a future husband's wish list! The kids made the whole equation seem much more complex and impossible to imagine any relationship being easy peasy.

Despite my serial dating during this time, I had not introduced a single one of my dates to my kids. Even the few guys whom I dated for a couple of months (no one had lasted longer than that) did not meet Morgan and Zach. I felt that it was not fair to the kids to introduce into their lives a male who may not stick around. Don't get me wrong; my little guy was all for me meeting someone, and he even took it upon himself to try to find dates for me. In fact, when Zach went off to sleep-away camp one summer, my first letter home from him explained that he had found me a boyfriend. I would later learn that this boyfriend was a twenty-two-year-old counselor. We never did facilitate that attempted love connection, but my son got an A for effort and dedication to the cause. Overall, I concluded that it was painful enough for me to go through this dating nonsense; the kids did not need to suffer as well.

I, however, repeatedly used my kids as an excuse to leave a date (thank God for small favors), but I vowed that I would not introduce a new person into our dynamic until I was sure. Although at this point "sure" about a relationship still seemed elusive and undefinable. I was not at a point in my life that I was sure about myself, let alone about any guy.

I guess now is as good a time as any to explain that I have not been the best decision-maker in my personal life. Professionally, give me your most complex legal problem, and I will solve it with confidence. Personally, I can barely buy a pair of jeans without overthinking it multiple times and likely eventually returning them. This is when you thank Nordstrom for their return-anytime policy. Overthinking is my curse and my superpower, all at the same time. Not a good combination when it comes to ease in life or relationships. I have to believe these love stories and their explanations that when it works, it really is easy.

The love stories emphasized that when the person is the right person, you have the same values and similar interests, which translates into easy. I can define the opposite of easy in relationships, and I readily admit to trying too hard to make something work. Whether it was a long-distance challenge or just a disconnect that was more local, I had tried too hard several times because I wanted the guy to be "it." Sure, happy couples go through hard times, but having to try so hard from the beginning was bad news. After hearing these stories, I was confident that I had not yet put my finger on anything close to "super easy" at any time during my postdivorce dating life.

The discussions continued to focus on how these couples tried to carry the ease into their marriages as they matured, focusing on helping their significant other or taking over things to make their partner's life easier. One older man about to be a grandfather explained that he knows how much his wife hates to cook, so he takes over dinner so she does not worry about it. Another husband shared that he and his wife both hate cooking, but he still agrees to take turns to share the burden and ease the lift for her, especially on days when she is in the office. Apparently, hating cooking was also a theme! Another man who was still in a dating relationship explained that his partner can read his mind. He knows when he needs closeness and when he needs space.

One of the best examples of carrying the ease into marriage was my observation that my dad always goes to the grocery store because my mom dislikes (actually despises) grocery shopping. I noticed this growing up, and while I thought it was unusual, based on the allocation of duties among my friends' parents, I did not think too much of it at the time. My dad is the extrovert anyway, so I was convinced that he had developed a deep friendship with the guy behind the deli counter and wanted to touch base with him weekly. Hearing my mom explain to me how much easier it made her life and how it reduced her stress made my heart happy. My dad used to do those kind things for me too—he always made sure my car was filled with gas once I was able to drive or asked me if he could pack me a lunch when I lived at home for a bit during my first year of law school. It's amazing how these little acts of love go such a long way. What I learned through these conversations was that taking on the parts of life that your partner dislikes will allow you to bring the ease into all aspects of your relationship.

This, however, requires you to know what the other person needs or wants, which requires a special level of connection and communication. The men I spoke with seemed to struggle a bit more with the ease of intuition and reading their partner's mind, but many of them felt completely comfortable asking the right questions to prevent disappointment. One of my favorite stories was a wife explaining that she had a drawer full of gifts from her husband. She told me in confidence that she did not like a single gift, and they had been married for over twenty-five years, yet she refused to donate them or throw them away because she knew he made the effort to pick them out. So these unworn trinkets had meaning for her in a different way...even if she would not be caught dead in that necklace! The origin of their love story also focused on the ease of their initial time together, as if they had known each other their entire lives. So even though he had no taste in gifts, she was grateful for the way he continued to try to bring so much joy to her life.

It appears that good relationships take some intuition and the ability to wait for the pairing that feels easy and right, as subjective as that feeling is. But the story told here is one that not only starts with ease but includes a real dedication to keeping it easy by lessening the burden of your person as your life progresses and you learn what it is that they love and what they dread. I think it is safe to say that life overall is not easy. The luckiest of us have easy days, weeks, months, or sometimes years, but hard will work its way in; it always does. When the relationship burden is shared, hard seems to be a little easier. I finally accepted that ease is an undefinable feeling that I had not yet felt, so I will just keep doing my puzzles and watching *Sex in the City* until that feeling comes my way.

Chapter 7

THE SEX OF IT ALL

Love is the beauty of the soul.
—Saint Augustine

I cannot talk about love and relationships without at least mentioning sex. Knowing that my kids are likely to read this book, I am keeping this chapter short and sweet (like me). I have never been shy when talking about sex, but during my project, I felt quite bold asking probably half of the people I chatted with about the role sex plays in their relationship. I could not bear to bring it up with Nana, my parents, or some of the other couples whom I admired but did not know as well. I saved this portion of my data collection for my close friends.

A few of the love-story targets actually said that they knew their significant other was "the one" when they first had sex. I only pried a bit into these answers, but it appeared that the connection and ease of their first time made the decision clear. A hairdresser explained he knew he had found his person after the first time he had sex with his partner, and a yoga instructor recounted the fact that she had sex with her partner too quickly, but she knew the minute they had physical contact that there was an interconnectedness she had not felt before. While I was still searching for answers that involved fireworks, I was enthralled by the openness and lack of spectacle that infiltrated the love stories.

One of my friends described the level of effort he put into making sure his wife enjoyed sex as much as he did. There was not much "mind-blowing" sex described. In fact, only one of the couples provided confirmation of mind-blowing sex. Some joked of past short-term relationships in which that rom-com level of sex occurred, but now, with their true partner, the love stories included details about ease, connection, and attention. I have to admit that I expected descriptions that included ripping clothes off or sparks flying everywhere; instead, I heard responses about fulfillment, even from the guys.

While I did not keep a tally, most of the couples I chatted with volunteered that they were having sex fairly regularly. Despite the fact that the vast majority of my data targets were in the midst of prime kid chaos with curious little monsters floating around, they confirmed that they were having sex at least weekly. Plus, several of the love stories exemplified good communication in every aspect of the relationship that included debriefing on sex, including likes and dislikes, what worked and what didn't, and even what their fantasies may be for nights when the kids slept at grandma's or the couples-only vacation to Mexico finally happened. There were a few complaints about not enough sex or a wish for sex more akin to what they used to engage in before having kids. Some explained that they had to schedule sex since life was too busy, but as a serial planner, I find that approach brilliant.

At the moment, the thought of replacing my vibrator with any type of regular thoughtful, two-way sex blows my mind. Yes, an actual human is preferred, especially one who cares about a true connection and your pleasure. But it's not just about the act of intercourse—it is about all the other romantic stuff as well. The hugging and kissing and petting. I was focused on the concept of whether feeling butterflies was a "thing," or was that just in the movies? If I am being honest, I have felt butterflies before, but only in connection with a "square peg in a round hole" situation, so I wondered if feeling butterflies was a warning sign rather than confirmation of success.

My research confirmed that feeling butterflies is a "thing," at least according to my younger, hipper couple friend and a few of the others. These love stories included recollections that meeting "the one" resulted in butterflies or at least a bit of a flutter in the tummy when they kissed the first time. One of my yoga pals claimed she still feels these so-called butterflies every time her husband kisses her, and they are about to have their ten-year wedding anniversary. While this is her first marriage, her husband was married previously. What a dream!

Butterflies aside, one of the best examples someone provided when I asked about sex and romance in her relationship was the feeling she gets when her husband holds her hand. Not in Target to make sure she does not buy everything in the store, but during a walk around the block or a night out. She adores it when he reaches for her hand unprompted, as if he wanted to be more connected to her at that very moment. The description she gave was one of comfort and support that brought a tear to my eye. I am a hands girl. The first thing I notice on a guy is his hands. I have to like his hands to go forward—weird maybe, but they symbolize something to me. Maybe strength? My tiny hands fit me, but I need my dates to have strong, well-kept hands. (P.S. Long nails on guys are gross.) So I could totally relate to the comfort and connectedness that holding hands could bring.

Over and over again, the love stories described the fact that skin-to-skin contact increased the intensity of their connection. Something that is easy to forget in our very busy lives when touching our phone seems to happen more often than touching our significant other. These conversations helped me to develop an even stronger appreciation for holding hands and physical touching. In fact, it appears that as far back as 1922, Hammett conducted one of the earliest studies on the benefit of touch and reported that rats that were handled less were more apprehensive and higher strung than rats that were petted. They were also six times less likely to survive (Hammett, F. S., *Endocrinology* 6, no. 2, 1922; 221–9).

More data to back up my analysis—even if it did involve rats, which I get is not sexy—tying in my recollection of those hug-ending fights, I was convinced about the value of touch, but it created a longing deep in my soul. I found a journal entry from August of 2009, where I contemplated this topic.

> *I have to let go of all this anxiety and all of this almost desperate urge to meet someone. I don't want any more horrible blind dates. I don't want to shop for a guy online anymore. I don't want to ask people if they know anyone to fix me up with. I want to have someone that longs to see me, longs to hold my hand, and longs to talk to me. Someone I can have that total intellectual conversation with, but then there is great sex that means something. I know that is a lot to ask for, but I feel like I deserve to be happy. Everyone does, but don't I deserve a happy ending after what I have been through? I need what I have never had, but I somehow, someway need to figure out how to stop longing for it all the time and how to start just living my life one day at a time without checking my phone or my email as if it is going to contain a magical message that will transform my life.*

While I was continuing to work on letting it all go, through these love stories I also was learning what true connection looks like. I started to be able to put a bit more definition on the elusive concept of love, but I was not yet convinced I understood it completely. For now, I would try to find peace in cuddling my dog, Oliver, and continue to long for butterflies, strong hands, and regular sexy time if I can find the guy to make it happen.

Chapter 8

BLENDING WORLDS

Love looks not with the eyes, but with the mind.
—**William Shakespeare**

One final theme was echoed during my interviews. Some love stories focused on the fact that their partner not only fit with them (round peg into round hole), but with their family and friends as well. A question I struggled with during my dating extravaganza and the few longer-term "dating-ships" (not quite making it to relationships) was whether and when to introduce the guy to my parents or my friends. Yet the stories from my subjects about how well a new love fit into their developed lives was astounding. One neighbor explained that her husband hit it off with her brother as if they had known each other forever. Another friend who had come out gay later in life, after being married to a woman, shared with me that his partner embraced his kids from the beginning and was genuinely interested in their happiness.

The "fitting into the family" theme was not as universal as the others, but it came up often enough to mention. For most people, family plays an important role in their life, so it makes sense that getting along with family would play an important role in their relationship. References to these answers led to several funny family stories and joint complaints about dreading Thanksgiving dinner or Passover Seder and being grateful for the gift of wine on these occasions. These mutual feelings kept the couple on the same team.

One of my favorite stories was a conversation I had with a husband who lost his father early in his life, well before he met his wife. He had a dynamo of a mom, but never had the father figure he so desperately longed for... until he got married. His father-in-law became his father in every way. I had another inspiring conversation with a friend who recalled the time when his mother was sick and dying of cancer. It was a long, awful process, but his wife became his mother's caregiver, even more so than his sister. His wife cooked for her, took her to doctors' appointments, sat with her during treatment, and became the one his mother could rely on. His now-late mother viewed his wife as a true daughter, and he would never forget the devotion and dedication she showed, which led him to love her in all new ways.

In those circumstances where families may not be around or a driving force in someone's life, friends who are family entered our discussions. I am a strong believer that "it takes a village," and there were a few trusted friends I vetted some of my potential dates with at times.

At some point around date seventy, you lose perspective, so second opinions are helpful. There were a few dates I did not feel comfortable sharing with my gal pals, so I knew right off the bat they were not going to be my forever. There were, however, one or two guys I introduced to friends during my dating marathon. While the guys tried to fit in, and my friends were open, there was not a true fit.

Instead, I showed up to mitzvahs, weddings, and other events solo. I was not a fan of getting a date for an event just to show up with a date, and trying to introduce a guy I hardly knew to friends, family, or work colleagues took too much energy. For a date, I much preferred meeting at a bar with the benefit of alcohol and the option of running for the parking lot at a moment's notice. Unfortunately, my life lacked that amazing guy friend who was willing to be my plus-one.

There were many times when I was getting dressed for an event and had to redo my makeup because I got teary-eyed thinking I had to go it alone…again. I shoved these feelings down, put on my big-girl underwear, and "sucked it up, cupcake"—one of my favorite expressions for my kids. The good thing is I had so many funny dating stories that I had my own stand-up routine for the cocktail-hour conversation. At least I was able to have a bunch of memorable slow dances with Zach when he was not running around with light-up wands or other mitzvah swag.

I was single and divorced before just about anyone in any of my friend groups. While I found some lovely divorced mamas to hang out with during this time,

I continued to try to fit into the OG groups as well. It remained hard at times. In looking back, I think I was jealous of their still-whole families and marriages, something I'm not proud of now. Plus, when couples went out together, they did not invite the divorced chick as a fifth or seventh wheel. These were the nights that I was thankful for a good rom-com or that I had TiVoed *American Idol*, a show that became a favorite for me and the kids to watch together.

Being someone who treasures friendships and the whole ride-or-die concept, I was uplifted by the way some of these happy couples explained that his friends became her friends and vice versa. There was a story about a sister-in-law becoming a best friend and the husband of his wife's BFF becoming his new go-to for golf. This, to me, was true integration and acceptance. Plus, I loved hearing about new couple friends being made together in the neighborhood, at school, and on the soccer field. One mom was so beyond grateful for her dance-mom parents who allowed her and her husband to survive the competition circuit with their two young girls. Another old friend talked about their neighborhood BFFs they made when they bought their first house together as a couple. These families shared everything together, from Fourth of July fireworks to New Year's Eve parties. Picture a literal village.

So it seemed that with friends and family, it went back to fit. Fitting into your life means fitting into your *whole* life; that includes family, friends, and sometimes even kids whom you do not share. It really should not feel as if you are squeezing into a pair of jeans that don't fit. It should feel more like the comfiest pants you own, the ones that fit like a glove and make you feel fabulous.

Another tangential theme arose from these conversations about family. Several people expressed that the thing they loved most about their significant other was that he was the best dad or the best grandfather or the best son. She was the best mom, the best sister, and a devoted daughter. Watching how their person interacted with the important people in their life allowed these couples to identify the qualities they admired most in the other person, and some mentioned that watching their spouse made them a better father or better son or better grandmother. While these descriptions went beyond the general discussion about fitting into a pre-existing network or building a joint network, it seems related because loving their person for how they showed up for others was a reason that couples stayed happy and appreciated each other.

These conversations convinced me that looking to my circle of support for their opinions and reactions was an essential part of my process to find true love, in the hopes that I would not be attending any more bat mitzvahs or weddings alone. After all, the love of your life is your family, and I was ready to take all that I learned from these love stories and create the family I longed to have in my life.

Chapter 9

THREADS

Love is composed of a single soul inhabiting two bodies.
—Aristotle

While my ad hoc science project generated excellent data, I found myself reviewing and analyzing these interviews over and over again for the one nugget of wisdom that would be the game changer for me. The one answer that would make love clear.

Yet there was no single answer. Upon every read and reread of my notes, these same themes came to life over and over again, albeit using different words or descriptions:

- He makes me my best self
- We take turns riding the waves
- We may fight, but I can't imagine life without her
- It was just incredibly easy to be together
- We prioritize our sex and physical connection
- He fits with my family and friends

As I attempted to extract these love stories, I did not ask questions with the aim of generating this data. I never asked, "Does he make you your best self?" or "How do you handle hard times?" Instead, I merely asked questions along the lines of "How did you know it was true love?" "When did you know you were in love?" or "How did he make you feel when you met him?" I did pry a bit into the sex and romance questions and occasionally ask if the couple ever fought.

There were a few times when both partners provided the exact same answer, even though I interviewed them separately. Those were the most joyful yet difficult interviews, as those were the ones that made me long for my future partner the most. These were couples who would have won that old *Newlywed Game*. They were clearly on the same page and had a deep connection that I felt at that time I would never be able to achieve.

While I am not a data analyst, I was able to quickly sort the responses and step back and consider what they meant. Finding the themes came with ease because although the individual answers were mushy and complex, the themes were woven through all the love stories like a beautiful tapestry, making them clear and concrete. Examining the responses allowed me to understand that we all feel and touch love a bit differently, but there are commonalities. Digging into the themes allowed me to release some of my own expectations as well. I could not expect love to be one way or the other, but I could look for these key elements in my future relationships. I could use the themes as a checklist to make sure a relationship was right or at least potentially a fit.

I suppose I could have completed my research without finding any themes, but I am comforted by the fact that in the almost fifty individuals I talked with about love, there was significant overlap in how they explained they knew they were in love and had found their partner for life. The descriptions they conveyed were personal to each husband, wife, or partner. The smiles were universally shared, but no two people described love the exact same way. No individual referenced all these themes, but many couples touched on multiple themes. Only one love target referenced all the themes during our discussion—a true standout.

I tried very hard to view these interviews through a lens of hope, but I would be lying if I dismissed this time as easy. The journey was very interesting, and it had joyful moments, but it was also challenging. While talking to my parents or my nana about their forty- or sixty-year-old loves was glorious, talking to the couples my age who had made the right choice at the right time and had true love to show for it was often hard for me to swallow. I was happy for all these people, but my journals reflect a lot of loneliness and hopelessness during this time. Hope is important, but it can also be hard to maintain.

Toward the end of my love-story quest, the responses remained original, but I started to hear the same type of information over and over again—the same themes. This is when I decided it was time to take my data and run, although I still was not sure where I was running. The love stories convinced me to spend time focusing on myself so that I could figure out how I could be the best partner and person for my take two. While I left the love stories behind for a while, I continued to move toward integrating these incredible themes of love into my life.

Part II
MY OWN LOVE STORY

Chapter 10

LOVE IN REAL TIME

Where there is love, there is life.
—**Mahatma Gandhi**

I am not sure if it was newfound wisdom from my research project or pure luck (maybe I am luckier than I originally thought), but I found true, real, once-in-a-lifetime love. The funny part is that when I found it, I did not have a single doubt about what it was and whether it was "it." At the point in my life that I met Will, I felt ready. I had processed my research, dated just about every single guy in Cleveland, and had both my professional and personal lives in a stable place.

On August 1, 2013, I ended my dating marathon and went on what would be my final blind date. In fact, I knew so quickly that I had gone on my final date that I made several people nervous, including my very dear yoga pal, Ann, who set us up. My love research, combined with my serial-dating experiences, allowed me to declare

Will my true love by our third date—frankly, if I am being honest, potentially on the first date. I would not call it love at first sight, but I would call it a miracle by some measures. Yet the black-and-white nature of my confidence about Will as my soulmate formed the bookends of what was a complex middle as we came into the relationship with two kids each, two ex-spouses, demanding jobs, and very different lives.

I met Will three years after I wrote part I of the book and a year after a women's mission to Israel where I placed a wish into the Western Wall, asking the universe to bring me the love of my life. I am not sure the wall brought me Will, but Ann did. As I continued to try to become my best self after hearing all the inspiring love stories, I doubled down on hot yoga, as nothing allowed me to free my mind and my heart like a hot-yoga class. Yoga was a saving grace for me during the single-mom years, and I forged a Front Row Crew (those of us who had to practice in the front row of the class to stay focused and avoid any distractions) with three other type-A yogis who included Ann. This Front Row Crew became a foundational circle in my life.

The Front Row Crew met for lunch and chats off our mats as well, but what the crew seemed to enjoy most was our Sunday-morning sweat fest in which I often showed up recalling the horrible date that I had the night before. I became a source of comedy for this crew—not in a bad a way, but in a way that the debrief between yoga breaths left me with support and hope.

The crescendo occurred when I had been dating a guy for a few months, although we had only seen each other formally a few times. It was one of those situations in which I had known him forever; there was "something" there, but when we got together, it never really worked (square peg in a round hole). Nevertheless, I was invited to a wedding of a client, and against my better judgment, I asked him to be my date, thus breaking my rule of not bringing dates to events. While I usually preferred to go alone, we had known each other for a long time and had gone on a few dates, so it seemed like a reasonable next step. He initially accepted, and then we ended up breaking off the relationship the week before the wedding.

When I called the bride to update her that I would once again be attending solo, she (who, by the way, is now divorced) told me that I would have an empty seat next to me because it was too late to make changes to her seating plan. At that time, this empty seat was incredibly symbolic of my life. After nine and a half years of being single, I went to that wedding fairly confident that the seat would be empty forever.

The recalling of the client-wedding story to the Front Row Crew was not the usual comedic Sunday-morning event. Instead, Ann was horrified. In fact, after our Saturday class the day of the wedding, she had offered up her husband as my date. I finally asked Ann if she knew anyone who may be interested in a fortyish lawyer with two kids. But the ask was something closer to "Please tell me you know sooooooomeeeeeonee????"

Ann reported back immediately that every time she saw this one guy, whom she hardly knew but interacted with in connection with work, she thought of me. He was older than I by almost ten years, which was breaking my dating rule at that time that I would not entertain anyone more than five years my senior. He was also not quite fully divorced, which broke yet another dating rule. I will explain later why you should not have too many rules.

I am not sure if it was despair or desperation, but I responded with a resounding "Yes!" Plus, his picture was pretty cute.

Ann then asked a local politician to join forces with her for Operation We Must Find Heidi a Match since she did not know Will quite well enough to ask him directly if he would be open to a random setup. The plan was set in motion during a meeting at Will's office in which Ann's politician pal asked Will, "Would you be interested in meeting a lawyer?" to which Will replied, "No, I have a good lawyer." Good progress was made from there, and Ann's accomplice left him with my number.

Will had not asked anyone out in twenty-seven years. Yes—twenty-seven. So he still believed that the only way to ask a person out was with a phone call, but he could not quite get himself to make that call. I later learned it had nothing to do with me and everything to do with his dating rustiness in general; he had even dialed my number and hung up. I eventually brought him into the twenty-first century with Ann's help by sending him an email. He replied immediately, and a cocktail encounter was scheduled.

I remember the night so clearly. Will picked the place in Chagrin Falls where we met. It had outdoor seating and views of the falls. Trendy but a bit romantic. At the time, I lived nearby, so it made sense. I wore a simple black dress with a belt around the waste and wedges. I still have that dress, although it would never fit me now. I was nervous, but never in a million years did I expect this guy to be the one.

I walked onto the patio talking on the phone to one of the members of my divorced-girlfriends troupe who was trying to instill a bit of game-day bravado in me as I started looking around the restaurant for him. He was not hard to find because he was sitting on the very first sofa by the entrance. Business-casual clothes and an adorable smile. My heart was definitely pounding louder than I remembered in quite a while. He drank a martini (dry with olives), and I had a glass of bad Riesling since this was still the time when I did not have any appreciation for good wine.

The drink turned into dinner and a recounting of our life stories. We moved from the sofa to an outside table and then to the inside bar once it started to rain. I remember someone telling me that rain is good luck, but all I cared about at that time was not looking like a wet rat on my first date. The funniest part was that we both used the word *partner* when talking about what we were looking for in life, and he was a CEO, not a lawyer. Thus, there was no confusion that we were talking about life partners, not law-firm partners. At the same time, he made it very clear that he never wanted to get married again. He was actually adamant. You will be pleased to know that I changed his mind by our third date.

The ground we covered during that first date was amazing. I remained my aggressive self, closing out that date by kissing him good night in the rain, which was rom-com-level romantic, and then texting him, as he had never really texted anyone (this was 2013!). By that time, I was way over waiting around for someone to text me or playing the dating-waiting games I had been playing for years, always losing. He immediately asked me out the following weekend via text—he was a quick study. I remember being disappointed that I would have to wait so long to see him again. I was heading to Chicago for a work trip, during which a dear friend encouraged me to just take the leap since this guy seemed so different. We ended up seeing each other the following night, after I returned to Cleveland, several days before our planned second date.

My initial text was the first of so many texts. I wish we had kept our phones from the first few months of the courtship, which was way before the good old iCloud. Weaving those texts together would have been emblematic of an epic love story. There were lots of trips back and forth between my house and his apartment. Intros to the kids and my family came quickly. I needed to make sure that he would fit in with my posse, just as the happy couples I interviewed had discussed. This was where I was reminded that when you know, you know, since I had promised myself no kid intros until I was "sure." In reality, I was already sure that Will was my guy, but our lives were still incredibly complex, and there were many steps in front of us before we could truly come together.

My personal love story is likely not very riveting, but what I realized very quickly after I met Will is that the things I learned throughout my research proved to be true and served as additional validation for this serial over-thinker. Plus, my own experience allowed me to put a bit of an additional twist on my research and understand it at a whole new level. My hope was that these combined experiences might provide some support or guidance to others wishing to add love to their lives.

Perhaps the most important thing that I learned through this long and complex process is that you never know when or where love may find you, but you do have to open yourself up to it. I mean be really open and not only in the small circle in which you live. Instead, you have to show the great big world that you are open and feel ready for it. My Front Row Crew was not my ride-or-die crew at the time—they were what you call social friends. While I adored them, and we shared lots of sweat and funny stories, they were outside of my standard little unit of peeps. They are my ride-or-die now, especially Ann. I realized, though, that explaining my desire to meet the right guy to those not in my immediate circle opened up all new possibilities for me. It is not only about an open heart, though—timing is so critical.

One of the craziest parts of my love story is that my husband is not from Cleveland; he only ended up here because of the real estate market crash of 2009 when he lost his job with a large developer and moved from Indy to Cleveland for a job here. At the time, Will felt angry about the circumstances, and maybe even a bit hopeless, trying to move two kids, one in middle school and one in high school, to a new city. While I love Cleveland, it is not the hottest destination for most, and our lake-effect snow is not much of a lure. The Rock and Roll Hall of Fame can only take you so far. Yet if all those terrible events did not happen, Ann would not have met Will, and he and I would not be together. The timing of these events changed my perspective overall on the whole concept of "when bad things happen." I now strongly believe that when one door closes, another opens. Thank goodness that his opened to Cleveland and eventually to me.

I spend a lot of time wondering what my life would have been like if I had met Will years ago and we had built a family together from scratch, rather than the *Brady Bunch* blended family that we have now. While I am confident that we are made for each other, the "other" that we are now is what makes it work so well. All those bad dates, sad moments, and lonely weekends, combined with the history that brought us to the day we met, make us who we are now and bring a whole new level of appreciation to the relationship. We both came from similar marriages (although his lasted a lot longer), kid relationships, and backgrounds. I am not sure if the moments that challenged us both in the past are what made us so right for each other, or if we were just born with similar perspectives about life, love, and the world and would have always been right for each other. It really does not matter. The important thing is that our worlds collided in the best way thanks to an intuitive yoga pal and a series of crazy events.

The three years between writing part I of the book and meeting Will were the busiest years I had in my dating life. I even went through a lunch-date membership that had me committed to the awkward process of a short lunch date multiple times each week. I swear every date was worse than the last. I actually took a bit of a dating cleanse after that process until I started back up again right before Will, which led to the whole empty-seat wedding fiasco. During my short-lived cleanse, I announced to the universe that I was done and would accept that my destiny was to be surrounded by friends and family rather than a husband or partner. Yet Fay's prediction haunted me. I am not a true believer in fortune-telling, but she seemed so sure; of course, I wanted to believe what she said. If I am being honest, believing Fay's premonition kept me going at times.

Even from the beginning of the process, I had a vision of what I hoped my future would look like and the kind of relationship I prayed I would find. In looking back at one of my journal entries from eight months into my separation from my ex-husband, I wrote:

> *What if my partner is out there somewhere and someone will take care of me. I know it is probably a dream that will never come true. I never pictured this in my life. But if I do not take this path [my divorce], I am not being honest with myself... I do not feel like I have started climbing*

*this mountain yet. The top is so far away. I cannot
see it.*

While it took several years before I was able to write in
that same journal again and to feel as if I was on my way
down the mountain, my urge to determine if my partner
was out there did not subside. Plus, I had spent so much
time gathering all this data; I could not let it go to waste.

One of the first processes I went through after meeting
Will was thinking constantly about all those interviews
and conversations that were parts of Project Love. I would
lie in bed at night, and the words of those love stories
would rush into my head. I truly felt that every single
theme that was discussed fit my relationship with Will.
Plus, after finally experiencing true love, I noticed various
nuances and revelations that actually enhanced my
research findings. I decided to put my own spin on my
data-collection exercise by considering each theme and
how it applied to my relationship and life with Will, as
well as how it did not apply to my previous attempts to
find the love of my life. My hope is that you can relate
to some of my epiphanies in your own journey to find or
treasure love.

Chapter 11

THE BEST ME

Perhaps the feelings we experience when we are in love represent a normal state. Being in love shows a person who he should be.
—**Anton Chekhov**

If you ask my kids what they hear the most from me (both the two whom I birthed and my two bonus kids), it is that they should not settle; instead, they should find someone who brings out the best in them, not someone they need to take care of or hope they will change.

When I was talking to all those husbands, wives, and partners years ago, the people who discussed the fact that their spouse brings out the best in them seemed to be the hardest concept for me to grasp at that time, even if it was my favorite theme. First, after completing my analysis of all those love stories, I felt pretty darn good about being single. I said *good*, not *complete*. Second, I was living a full life between work and my village. My parenting needed a tune-up here and there, but that is another book. During the time of my interviews, my professional life was also thriving. I became very devoted to supporting women in the law, and I worked with others to launch initiatives locally, regionally, and nationally in which women could come together to network and find support. This work gave me energy and enthusiasm. In fact, after much therapy, I was confident that I could live my best life as a strong, independent single woman.

What I did not understand is, when you do not have the partner and connection that these love stories highlighted, you do not know what you are missing. You do not even realize that you might not yet be your very best self. Let me give you a basic example. I have a husband who knows art, politics, literature, music, and travel better than most of the people who were in my life before him and, frankly, since him. I never had a real appreciation for these things until I met him, as he opened my eyes up to all types of new culture and beauty. I actually took my first trip to Europe with him after we had been dating about a year. Yes, I was forty-three and had never been to Europe. It was not in the cards for me before this time, but neither was reading the *New York Times* on Sunday, so I actually could understand the political climate around the globe, rather than my old single habit of reading *People* magazine and *US Weekly*, although those did stay in the rotation for a while. I am most definitely a better, more well-rounded person with his influence.

While those examples may sound a bit fancy (I realize I am part of a privileged few), my husband grew up lower middle class, just like me, and very independent. Picture him mowing the lawn weekly in middle school, but he had parents who instilled these values and interests in him due to their professorial and educational roots. But Will's ability to make me my best self is by no means limited to material things. Even more significantly, what I did not realize before was that when you are with someone whom you truly connect with at all levels, you want to do your best and be your best every day for them. Anytime I accomplish anything at work, I want to call Will. I strive for success so he will continue to be proud of me. When he gives me a compliment or applauds something I have completed, it brings me true joy. He tries every day to make the world a better place, as cheesy as that sounds, so I want to do the same.

I know I have rubbed off on him as well, bringing him into my Cleveland community where he has seen firsthand the value of the support a village can bring. I have shown him what it means to show up for people and to have friends who are family. I have instilled additional Jewish morals and values in Will and my bonus kids (though they already had a wonderful foundation of these) with celebrations and gatherings, and I have shared my passion for diversity, equity, inclusion, and belonging.

But one of the best examples is likely the fact that I think we would both say we are better parents now. We have different parenting styles, but the merger of the two styles—and, especially for me, Will's calm and strategic views since he thinks parenting is a long game—has shifted my focus and tremendously improved the way

I parent my kids. Having a partner to discuss kid issues with and to help find solutions is priceless, and I hate to tell you that even adult kids have many issues while they work on "adulting." Though we both felt so much love for each other's kids, sometimes it was easier for the parent who did not birth the child to identify problems and even solutions. I guess that is called perspective, but it can be hard to take if you look at this perspective as a criticism of your parenting or a negative observation about your child. We were able to quickly get past these challenges. The therapist for a few of our boys, whom we both treasure, told us that our opinion on the other spouse's kids will always matter as long as it comes from a place of love. There was plenty of that. I truly believe a kid can never have enough people who love them, so the stepdad stepping up has been a gift.

I do know what not bringing out the best looks like. I dated someone for a few months off and on when I first became single again after my divorce. It was someone I met online, another lawyer, whom I likely would not have interacted with outside of the online nonsense. Picture lots of passion, but I learned early on that there was no honesty. His Match.com profile said he was fully divorced, but he was not; instead, he was just separated. I was able to figure the truth out fairly quickly, but for some reason, I hung on a bit. I wish I could say I was just trying to have fun, but I have to admit that I was once again trying to make something work that would not work. If you do not start a relationship with a foundation of truth, it will be a bust, no matter the level of attraction. In looking back at my journals, I was miserable during the short time period I dated this guy, always guessing how he felt and wondering if this was as good as it gets. Well, it's not. Sometimes the search for love and your person pushes you to ignore your gut reaction. What was blaring to me in these journal entries is that this guy was bringing out the worst in me—self-doubt, sadness, fear, etc.—the opposite of what my happy couples talked about.

One thing I have never doubted is that Will is always honest with me, and he has adopted our family motto—well, my motto I drilled into my kids—"All truth, all the time." The foundation of trust we built from day one during our oversharing has just continued to expand over time. I am also continuing to grow and mature in positive ways as our relationship becomes deeper and stronger. I have several greeting cards that I saved, as we used to love to exchange cards, in which Will also thanks me for making him a better person. Hard for me to take credit for that accomplishment because I think he was born the best, but it is nice to know that the feeling is mutual.

The moral of the story is that it is just as important to know who a real partner is not as it is to find your true other half. At the end of the day, I am my best, most-developed self with my husband. Something I strived for ever since I heard over and over again during my interviews how these truly in-love couples bring out the best in each other.

Chapter 12

EFFORTLESSLY US

Love is born into every human being; it calls back the halves of our original nature together; it tries to make one out of two and heal the wound of human nature.
—Plato

Picture this. I walked into the back room of a popular bar with a friend who was also single. There was a small group of women standing around in a cluster and many guys sitting behind long tables. While I am a proud Jew and even tried JDate on several occasions, this was next level. This was Jewish Speed Dating. Somehow, my mother convinced me to go. I regretted it from the moment I arrived.

The guys ranged from thirty-five to sixty-five, many had never been married, and others I am pretty sure had not been in public since the nineties. We were given a sheet of paper since apps weren't a thing yet, and the speed-dating guide instructed the women to jot down the names of the guys they were interested in getting to know better.

By this time, my friend bowed out and went to the actual bar—well, to be honest, she ran to the bar. Since I follow through on literally everything, I was off to the Jewish Speed Dating races.

The buzzer rang, and I spent my first five minutes with a guy who lived at home with his mother. Next! The buzzer rang again, and the next guy was still finishing up college even though he was quite a bit older than I. Next! The buzzer rang, and I moved on to the next guy, who asked me why I was not putting anyone's information down on the paper I was instructed to fill out. "I just need time to process," I explained, but I was actually thinking that if these are the only Jewish guys left in Cleveland, it was time to move.

After handing back a blank paper to the organizer, I headed to meet my friend at the bar. We ended up chatting with a guy who claimed to have attempted to join speed dating, but unfortunately for him, it was full. He seemed charming and funny and sort of cute, or in retrospect, maybe it was as compared to the other potential bachelors I had just visited with for five minutes each. I ended up giving him my number.

He texted me the next day, and we met at a sushi bar for wine and a futomaki roll later that week, where I learned that he had taken the bus to meet me because "his car was in the shop." I will cut to the punch line that it ended up that this "catch" had a DUI and later tried to literally jump me when he asked for a ride home (do NOT ever agree to drive a date home). This fiasco turned out to be my first and last speed-dating experience and the last time I picked up some rando at a bar.

The sushi guy definitely did not fit like an old sock, as that older man explained when he shared his love story during my research project. But that analogy did not really work for me since I throw out my old socks. My equivalent instead was that I was searching for a prince with a glass slipper that would fit me perfectly. This probably relates back to my general obsession with shoes. Will has even come to embrace my obsession and supported my recent build-out of the closet to accommodate my shoes. While I do not believe in fairy tales, I do believe that there has to be a "fit" in lifestyles, outlook, and morals. A good relationship really does need to feel comfortable, like a Birkenstock, rather than a stiletto, or even better an UGG boot! When I met Will, he truly was holding the proverbial glass slipper, and it was a size 6!

Will fit into my world so well immediately, which brought me so much comfort. The comfort seemed to initially be derived from the fact that I quickly learned that our brains worked in the same way. We now joke that we have the "same brain," which our kids like to tease us about all the time. We just tend to look at challenges, goals, and celebrations in the same way, especially challenges. We weirdly even have the same dreams at night. I would love someone to analyze that! You know the one where you are in high school, and you cannot remember your locker code, you are late for class, and you miss the test and fail the class. At least I am dressed in my dream, as Will tends to be naked in his version, so I am not sure what that is about.

Comfort can also come from enjoying the same types of things that allow you to connect at different levels. A favorite spot for both of us is dinner and a cocktail at a great restaurant bar. We also are obsessed with travel and our adorable first joint child, our rescue dog, Felix. We love watching certain shows together, especially *Ted Lasso* and *Mad Men*. Our walks together are heaven, and we both love dreaming about where we can retire and listen to the ocean.

But this does not mean that feeling comfortable has to include a love for ALL the same things, people, or activities. As with everyone I interviewed, the happiest couples included individuals with their own identities and interests. Will only went to hot yoga with me once during the beginning of our dating days, which he admits was part of his overall strategy to woo me. He now would not be caught dead in that hot, sweaty room that, as I explained earlier, is my heaven.

Will's heaven is a Dead and Company concert, and while I am happy to attend as a loyal spouse, I just don't get that music or those twenty-minute drum solos. I am a *Coffee House* on Sirius kind of girl. Will loves sci-fi movies, and I am all about the rom-com. He binges thrillers, and I cannot get enough Bravo (*RHONY* is my fave). Will loves the water, all kinds of boating, and backpacking. I pretty much hate boats because I am not a good swimmer, and while I am up for a great hike, I don't enjoy carrying things, and any version of a tent is a nonstarter.

I don't think it is fair to discuss fit without addressing the kids. When second marriages occur, one of the most challenging things is fitting in a way that does not risk your primary goal of continuing to parent your own kids as your number one priority and making the kids feel as if they fit too. Our situation did not come together overnight, but we have both been lucky and strategic in integrating our kids so that we all fit together as a real family while honoring the origins and original family structure of each of the kids. As I said before, you can never have too many people who love you, and we both have come to love our four completely.

Our integration took time and patience and had many challenges, but what is important is to have a significant other who is open to and embraces your kids. We have several friends in the same position. Those second marriages that are working best are those in which the stepparent is respectful of the OG and considers the kids he or she did not birth as an extension of their own, even if they are grown. Those couples who are in a do-over and do not have this view, but instead see the kids as a separate entity rather than an integrated unit, have had lots of challenges that can add stress to what otherwise may be a perfect match.

While the kids add a layer to the fit and Will and I have our independent likes and interests, the comfort I feel when he puts his hand in mine or listens to me intently is second to none. Just hearing him breathing when he is sleeping brings me joy in a way that I can hardly explain, although I can do without the snoring. I feel as if we physically fit together, and there is no more calming place for me than when my head is lying on his chest. He also knows how to support me like no other (and continues to improve over time). In fact, the longer we are together, the more we learn what the other needs and appreciates and are able to understand when a hug or smile is needed rather than a fix to the problem.

When we finally found each other, that cheesy theme of finally coming home came to life. We eventually sold our old homes and bought a home together to further integrate the kids and our families. It just felt comfy, cozy, and peaceful with Will, even though selling our homes was anything but that. I think if someone checked my heart rate when I am sitting next to him, versus when I am not, they would notice a huge difference. He literally is my weighted blanket. I am grateful for that EVERY... SINGLE...DAY.

Our love story traces those that discussed comfort and fit. We have been able to bring comfort to each other in so many ways. Coming together and bringing our kids together allowed us to find the fit that we were always missing before and to build the home together we had both dreamed about for so long.

Chapter 13

PERFECT BALANCE

*Love takes off the masks that we fear we cannot
live without and know we cannot live within.*
—**James Baldwin**

By now, you know I am not a huge fan of water. I love looking at it. Nothing is more peaceful, which makes sense since I am a Pisces, but a challenging swim incident at day camp when I was young left me scarred for life. Yet my old therapist and so many of the couples I chatted with talked about riding the waves of life together and taking turns pulling each other up. This visual appeared in my dreams for a long time, as it became a true goal for me.

The key piece in the visual is that no one person is the wave rescuer all the time. There is no one person who is the rock. It has to be a shared obligation/opportunity; you take on that challenge when the other person needs you to do so. Basically, the mentality is "It's your turn to throw me the life raft. I got you next time."

I am not qualified to say that any one of the themes that I found during my research is more important than the others. I also am not going to say that every relationship has to have all the themes I discussed with my subjects, but I will go out on a limb and assert that this wave riding is the most important theme for me. Probably because I have historically been a caretaker and have engaged in relationships all my life in which I tended to be constantly pulling up the other person from these theoretical waves, which is not a great thing when, like me, you cannot swim. It gets exhausting and creates an unhealthy dynamic. It took a lot of therapy for me to recognize this flaw in my relationship-selection process.

The reason I would argue that the concept of taking turns pulling each other up is the one foundational piece in a relationship is because you never know how big or tall or challenging those waves will be during the course of your relationship. And, man, oh man, we have had some whoppers come our way since I met Will. During a wedding, you commit to each other that you will support each other in sickness and health and all those things, but do you even really think about what that might mean? While the early days of our courtship included both of Will's parents passing away within six months of each other, some complex kid issues and a few minor surgeries for me, we learned very quickly what it meant to count on and completely support each other. What we did not know is that our reliance on each other would be tested at all new levels starting in 2020, when we were coming up on our fifth wedding anniversary.

In the span of two years, we dealt with both COVID and cancer. Two C words I hope to never hear again, and I never really imagined would enter our lives in the first place. First, COVID struck on my fiftieth birthday. Literally, the World Health Organization (WHO) declared the pandemic on March 11, 2020—the day I turned fifty. Not sure who I pissed off in this karmic universe, but it must have been a doozy.

As we all know, the wonderful pandemic led to us being trapped in our homes for longer than we care to remember. For Will and me, we had two kids still at home (a high school junior and a recent college grad), and the other two returned quickly from Italy and Germany, where they were both having the times of their lives abroad. Reverse empty nesting was not in the plan, nor was spending our days wiping groceries down with Clorox and building a home gym.

If you really want to test a relationship, lock yourselves in a house for months, watching CNN updates twenty-four seven about a deadly pandemic, with four kids ranging from seventeen to twenty-three. What was so crazy about this process was that we actually became closer and began to enjoy our full-time days and nights together, even with the overloaded Wi-Fi. We treasured our walks in the neighborhood and cooking together every night, which is likely why I now hate to cook. We celebrated our fifth anniversary on a card table in our bedroom with candles and some type of takeout that I decided was safe enough to eat—after we wiped down the containers, of course. We exchanged handmade cards and reminded each other how grateful we were that we had each other during this scary, unusual mess.

Just as the vaccines emerged and life seemed to start to become a bit more normal, Will was diagnosed with early-stage breast cancer. (PSA: Men can get breast cancer too!) He found the lump in his breast himself by a stroke of luck. The good news is he is not one of those guys who refuses to go see a doctor. It is the one time in our entire relationship that he has kept something from me because he knew how stressed I was already with all that we had going on at that time. Will did end up telling me about the possibility of cancer right before he went in for the final diagnostic ultrasound that confirmed he had it. Thank goodness he finally told me, as we were able to share the pain and stress and anger of receiving that information together. Although, to be completely honest, I did not even go to the ultrasound appointment with him because the chance of this lump being cancer was so incredibly low, as men are only 1 percent of all breast cancers. He assured me that the test was just a confirmation that it was a benign nothing, so I focused on my work-from-home gig until he called me with the devastating news.

We spent the next seven months going through a mastectomy followed by chemo and radiation. I would venture to say that those were the hardest days of my life, and I know the hardest ones for Will. Harder than the divorce and harder than raising kids as a single mom. Seeing the person you love more than life itself go through such horror is unparalleled to any other life experience. One of my most vivid memories is sitting at the hospital when he was in surgery for his mastectomy. This is the time you find out if there is lymph-node involvement, and, of course, you never know what they will find once they open someone up. I felt as if I were having an out-of-body experience, as the only other time I was that afraid was when I gave birth to my first child eight weeks early.

Combine that visual with the fact that I am a person who wants to fix every problem, but this was a problem I had zero control over and certainly could not fix. At every step of the way, we had to just wait for the data to find out how bad it was, what was the chance he would recover, and how he would fare with the next steps. During the entire process, it was my turn to be the one to pull us up over this incredibly large wave. The good news is we live in a great city for medical care, and I have a ton of strong connections that allowed me to take some control and at least expedite the process.

Will is a fighter and an optimist, though, and so I did all I could to share the pain, provide support, and follow the motto "The only way out is through." Since it was still during the height of COVID, we could not leave our house at all except to go to the doctor for appointments or the hospital for treatments because his immune system was basically gone. So "together time" was an understatement. It was a time when I had to learn to distinguish when he needed me and when he needed space. I had to learn the ways in which I could help him the most, and I had to be careful with my role because I did not want to force Will to lose control of his own health process.

I put a lot of the pandemic out of my mind. I have very good memories of times together as a family, but they are somewhat faded, and others are just forgotten. Cancer, though, I remember it as if it were yesterday, and each and every step still seems so vivid to me. Weirdly, I have a few positive memories of those times. Mostly the fact that I made Will walk twice a day during treatment, no matter the weather, as we received very good advice that moving around would help. I loved those walks together, even though I sometimes had to push him. We had such wonderful talks and shared our feelings, and then at other times we were silent but so darn together.

The problem with that wave was that I felt from the moment that I met Will that he was just too good to be true. I will admit that I am a glass-half-empty kind of person sometimes and am constantly waiting for something bad to happen, so this scare did not help that fear. There is not a day that passes that I don't think about that ugly enemy coming back. I hope and pray that is a wave we never have to ride again. I also recognize that many are not as lucky, and there are diseases and health issues that require someone to truly care for the person they love long-term.

I am not recounting all this awfulness to bring sadness to what is supposed to be a happy and joyful summary of what love looks and feels like, but life is not only trips to Paris and martinis on a patio at an outside bar. I still wonder how I would have possibly made it through COVID PW (pre-Will, as I like to say). I would have lost my mind completely. I have such empathy for all the single parents who were so alone during such a hard time.

The moral of this chapter is that we don't know what is going to pull us underwater. What we do know is that we will go under at some point, so when we reach up to grab a hand, are you sure that hand will be there so you don't have to rescue yourself? As I explained before, I am a girl-power, independent woman, but we all need support at one point or another.

After finding Will and realizing I was able to let go of things on some level, I wanted to call the marriage therapist I visited so long ago with my ex-husband to say, "See, I told you so—I can let someone take care of me." I think we all can let someone take care of us if we have a person who is willing to and if we trust our partner. Nothing feels better than being cared for by someone, especially when life feels desperate or scary.

But being cared for by just anyone is not what works. At one point in my dating days, I was in such a funk, and someone set me up with surgeon. He seemed like a nice enough guy, and we went to grab dinner. I had zero attraction to him—looks, personality, you name it. Unlike some dates where I used my young kids as an excuse to run, I decided that I needed to give this one a try and stayed through dinner. Several glasses of wine helped. He seemed like the kind of guy who would be reliable, dependable, and, well, a rock. He had grown girls whom he had strong relationships with, and he was Jewish, which for me was important. He called me the next day to ask me out again, and while I had many friends pushing me to keep trying, I just could not do it. I was honest with him and told him that I did not think it was a good fit. I was not a fan of leading people on and may have often been a little too honest and direct. While today this same guy is someone else's rock, he was not mine. So just being a rock is not enough on its own; the person has to be *your* rock.

Once you have the right fit and a foundation of comfort and trust, there has to be an understanding of what it takes to support each other through life's challenges. Even good swimmers can go down and need a hand to pull them up. I am so grateful that I found the perfect hand and a really good swimmer.

Chapter 14

FEEDBACK AND FORGIVENESS

*Life without love is like a tree
without blossoms or fruit.*
—**Khalil Gibran**

Of all the themes, I had the hardest time relating to the ones about fighting and hearing the love stories that included times of anger and resentment. Will and I had hardly fight; he virtually never makes me angry. Now, I don't want all of you hating on me since I feel as if I am still on my honeymoon almost ten years later. I am just being honest. Will and I do, however, experience a feedback loop regularly enough for it to be a thing for us. Basically, one of us gets angry or frustrated about something. This leads to the other person getting angry and frustrated, which just escalates the whole thing, and the bad feelings circle in a loop. This scenario usually only happens when there is a lack of communication or when one of us is holding back from sharing our true feelings, for fear the other may get hurt.

In the love stories, I could easily relate, though, to the people who explained that, no matter how angry they got, they never wanted their significant other to leave. Hey, I am not even thrilled when Will has to go to Chicago overnight. Even when we are in a bad feedback loop or when we have had a few fights, nothing scares me more than the thought of Will leaving. Well, there are probably one or two things related to my children, but for the most part, I need Will by my side. It is healthy to disagree and fight, and my research seemed to conclude that the best couples know how to fight well and also when it does not make sense to hold on to grudges or regurgitate past issues. It becomes essential to learn how the other person communicates, what makes them tick, and how sometimes just listening is what is important.

Listening is a skill set I have had to develop over the years. As an admitted fixer, my first reaction to any problem is to try to solve it. In fact, my day job is to foresee the problem and find a solution before the problem even occurs. My therapist likes to say that I am a heat-seeking missile, and not in a good way. One of the things Will has taught me is that sometimes he just needs to vent, and, man, he can vent like no other. During those times, he does not need me to solve his problem; he just needs me to listen and validate his feelings. This was an epiphany for me, and as soon as I adjusted my response, things worked so much better between us. Sometimes it is just as important to develop a process that works for both of you and adjust it over time.

On his side of things, when we were first got together, Will often held back. I think it was a combination of not wanting to upset me and not being used to sharing at the level I was looking for. Sometimes these bottled-up feelings caused issues. We have since found ways to get past this dynamic, so we have had significantly fewer fights. It also helps that our kids are grown-up and out of the house, so we have fewer day-to-day parenting discussions and potential disputes.

When I interviewed both my parents and my nana, they all conveyed positions that seemed to be aligned with mine. I have witnessed some bad fights between my mom and dad. Still, almost sixty years later, they are each other's very best friend and support system. Nana conveyed that she usually got her way with her late husband. She did admit that they had a few fights here and there, but never did she envision them not being together. It was truly "until death we do part" for them.

We all have bad days, bad weeks, and even bad years. No one is perfect, and we all make mistakes, so it's only logical that mistakes are made in even the strongest relationships. It's how we address these mistakes, communicate about them, and rectify them that seems to matter most. One of my favorite work terms is *expectation management*, and it seems to work in life as well since sharing feelings in order to manage expectations allows couples to continue to build on what is already a solid foundation.

The concept of never wanting someone to leave you that these couples talked about also helped me know when a relationship was not right because I was sometimes relieved when I broke it off. The situation that comes immediately to mind in this scenario is the one I mentioned at the beginning of the book—the relationship that had me yearning for answers that were not forthcoming. My journals came in handy when reflecting back, as there were too many questions I kept asking myself while we were dating. It's not that we fought much; we did not. He was also a bit broken at the time as he had lost a job and was looking for another, and I was trying to help fix the situation, of course, since I was still stuck in my old patterns. I was convinced by the time I was dating this person that my inner voice was completely broken. But he did seem to have more potential than most. I vividly recall agreeing to end the relationship right after a disagreement about Halloween costumes. While it took me a few days to process and get over the disappointment of another failed dating scenario, I was not sad that we had split because I knew it was the right decision. In looking back, I credit my love research with giving me the perspective and insight to know that it was time to move on and cut my losses.

I am now that crazy wife who cannot wait for Will to return from work each day. I sometimes long for the days of COVID when we were together all the time, which I know many will think is insane. I treasure our vacations when even our twenty-four-seven days together are never long enough. I dream about retirement; I am hoping that we can then sit drinking coffee together, staring at the ocean, until it is time to drink wine together, staring at the ocean, minus a midday yoga class for me and a boat ride for him. While I hope to continue our streak of having very few fights, I am 100 percent all in on the theme that he can never leave me, and we will continue to work on avoiding that nasty feedback loop.

Chapter 15

POT LIDS

Every heart sings a song, incomplete,
until another heart whispers back.
—Plato

In looking for the ease that the love stories echoed, I concluded that ease needed to be present even at the beginning of a relationship. I recently had a conversation with my youngest who at the time was a junior in college dating someone he really seemed to like. He, however, was constantly waiting for her to text him, communicate with him, or prioritize him. He is my kid, so he does tend to be an overcommunicator. It did not take long, however, to realize that the relationship was not going to work. While I could tell from the beginning, it took him a bit to get there and realize that they were not connecting when it should be easy. You cannot force it. So even when the fit seems like a good one, or you want it so badly you are pretending it's a good fit, a solid connection also has to be easy peasy, lemon squeezy (cheesy, I know).

My grandmother Lilly had a famous saying, "There is a lid for every pot." She reminded all of us quite often of this premise as she saw her sisters as well as some of her nieces struggle with love. She also liked to remind me that when there is a match, the goal is to save four people from being miserable. This seemed like great advice, especially since before I became an uber-organized, crazy person with the pot lids stored directly on top of each of the pots so they could not possibly be lost, I was constantly searching for the right lid every time I cooked. But you know the feeling when you find the right lid—it fits perfectly. You don't have to jam it or push it. I had been jamming and pushing the pieces of so many relationships before Will.

One of my favorite stories is how easy it was for Will and me to travel to Columbus for Will's birthday when we had only been dating for three weeks. We decided that a little getaway would be fun. Ann, my yogi guru match-maker, was frantically texting me that it was *TOO SOON*. Yet this ended up being the time when overaggressive Heidi told Will she loved him. What is amazing about a road trip, though, is you need to figure out how you can find something to talk about every minute of the two-and-a-half-hour drive. Yet even at just three weeks in, Will and I felt just as comfortable in silence, listening to music, as we did in sharing more about our past, our kids, our goals, and what looked like a joint future even at this point. Will stopped at the store prior to picking me up and stocked up on enough snacks for a ten-hour trip, none of which we ate. Such a thoughtful gesture…or maybe I looked hungry at that point in my life, which most definitely is no longer true.

We were in the "still getting to know each other" phase at this point, but spending thirty-six hours with someone you have known for only three weeks could go bad fast. Once I crafted a plan to poop in the lobby bathroom instead of the room, I was greatly relieved (no pun intended), and we were able to share some of our oldest secrets and lots of quality time together. It truly was easy. So much so that we have basically been together every day since that trip, which was followed by many more. Traveling can be complex, and not everyone travels well together, but our happiest times are wandering and exploring or just lying by a pool, looking at the beach. We kept the hotel key card from this first trip and every room key card since that risky Columbus adventure. Will claims, in retirement, he is going to design a piece of art with them. We shall see.

You know when a relationship is not easy. I have many memories of trying too hard to make things work, many of which I have shared already. Sometimes physical chemistry does not translate into life chemistry. These types of connections, instead, should be left as one-night stands or other terms I will not use since my kids will read this book. I have had one-night stands, although very few of them. I am not very good at connecting on such a superficial level, even in the most desperate of times.

What wasn't easy was my first postdivorce fling with my teen-camp crush who had grown up to be a wine distributor. During the twenty-plus years we fell out of touch, he had gotten married, had triplets, and grown a crazy business. Plus, he lived across the country. After Facebook allowed us to reconnect, and we figured out we were getting a divorce at the same time, we decided that a camp reunion was in our cards. He had not changed much and was still the same sweet, fun guy from my sophomore year of high school. We continued to try to date a bit, but our meetups were only trips, and no real life was involved. While it was likely what I needed at that time, it was not easy or right. We did drink some damn good wine though.

There was a point during this endurance-dating exercise when I was convinced that I would never find easy, but sadly I was basing my conclusion on an interaction with a horse. Two of my best friends took me to a spa in Arizona to regroup after yet another failed dating scenario. Picture June in the Southwest—105 degrees and lots of women in robes. My smart gal pals opted to sit by the pool and drink all day while I did yoga, made pottery, and signed up for horse therapy that claimed to be life-changing for what I think was the small cost of $500. The horse adventure started when I joined the twenty other sad, desperate women in the spa's van. We headed out to the horse barn, where the so-called horse whisperer convinced us all to share our sad stories. Man, my story was the best of the bunch. He then attempted to counsel us that in order to grow and move and leave our baggage behind, we needed to trust the horse fully and completely. Once we felt this "connection" with the horse, the horse would allow us to pick up his foot to clean his hoof. Mr. Horse Guy claimed that this process was reflective of how we each interacted in our current relationships, and he stressed the need to provide good vibes that showed both trust and confidence. Of course, to make me feel even worse, several of the women went right up to the horse and had a hoof in hand in a matter of minutes.

While the actual event remains a tad bit blurry in my head from all the tears that I shed, suffice it to say that the dang horse would not move for me. I mean, did not budget an inch. It was as if they had glued its hoof to the ground. I swear he was looking at me and saying, "F*** you, you crazy bi***." At one point, the therapy dude did get the horse to move a bit, but I decided then and there that if relationships were that hard, I was done. Either I had no trust, or horses hate me, or both. It took me the rest of the spa vacation to recover from that travesty, while my girls could not stop laughing that I actually felt my experience with this creature would dictate the rest of my love live. I was convinced that if I could not shake this horse's hoof, there would be no love for me in the future.

This was definitely during a time when I was looking for some external sign or input from the universe as to what direction I was supposed to head. My friends understood this quest, and my birthday party that year included a visit with a tarot-card reader. This is likely because I was constantly talking about Fay, so my pals were convinced that doubling down on positive predictions may serve me well. I have my journal entry from my party on March 7, 2010, to remind me exactly what the tarot-card reader predicted. The main prognostication of this lovely lady was that I would indeed meet my soulmate, but not yet. Instead, it would take about two years, and then it would happen by chance when I was out with friends. He would be a guy who seemed a bit rough around the edges at first, but I would be one of the first people to call him on that. She advised me that the relationship would start slow, but it would be a great one. Urging me to have patience, she explained that I would not be interested if I met him in the near future, and I could not rush it because I needed more time to evolve and grow. In the interim, I would date two different men, one who was materialistic and too worried about his career and a second who seemed like a good communicator on the outside but deep down was not. At the conclusion, she repeatedly reminded me that I needed to forgive myself.

Weirdly, Madam Tarot Card was pretty spot-on about both forgiving myself, something I was working on at the time, and the two guys I would date a bit in the interim. Otherwise, she missed the mark big-time. She was off by about a year and way off by the manner in which I would meet the love of my life and what his overall qualities would include. Nevertheless, the card reading served its purpose, as it gave me hope at a time I needed it. I admit I spent countless hours lying in bed, trying to figure out what "rough around the edges" really meant.

What easy looks like to me, though, is probably not what easy looks like to you. It is truly a feeling as if you finally have come home. You can be attracted to someone, have amazing conversations, and like the same things, but still the relationship is hard. That means it is probably not the right one. Please do not misunderstand me, as I do not think that relationships are easy. That is the understatement of the century. They take hard work every day. You have to learn and grow together and prioritize each other, but if it is not easy from the get-go, during the initial "madly in love, hot and heavy, cannot get enough of you" days, then it is likely not right and will only get harder and more complex from there.

This is also as good a time as any to talk about physically fitting together, and I do not mean lifting weights or running on the treadmill. I mean fitting in a way that makes sex work well. There will be no Heidi and Will sex chapter (sorry to our kids, who I am sure are super disappointed), but I think it is important to say that a relationship also has to work and be easy in bed. While I endorse a process that takes a bit of time to find your groove, if that initial kiss does not do it for you, I am pretty sure the other pieces of the puzzle will never come together. I still get the best feeling when Will kisses me or holds my hand. No more details beyond that though. Overall, it is no secret that sex is a huge part of a relationship, and I learned that those who have the best ones certainly make time for sex, no matter what.

Beyond sex, ease in the relationship should include physical touch in a way that enhances connection and, even in the hardest times, brings you closer. This reminds me of a *Today*-show episode. I am a huge fan, and it is my life goal to chat with Hoda and Savannah. This particular episode aired around Valentine's Day in 2020. Hoda interviewed couples who had been together for more than thirty years; several had been together for sixty-plus years. Hashtag #Goals is an understatement, but what

I recall most clearly is what one older couple said in their interview. When Hoda asked them, "What is your secret to staying together and being happy for more than sixty years?" the husband quickly said, "We sleep naked." The wife nodded. He went on to explain that their skin-to-skin contact every night enhances the connection they have to each other. This bonding keeps them close and on the same page when the craziness of life gets in the way. I took this as very sage advice, and it stuck in my head. It's up there in my best-practices checklist, next to the advice I obtained during my research to just go hug your significant other if things get too heated.

I believe in Grandma Lilly's lid-and-pot wisdom. Sometimes the lid seems to be missing and never to be found, but it's out there. When you find the lid that fits with ease, it is a gift from the universe that should be cherished with lots of time for connection and a definite avoidance of horses and tarot-card readers.

Chapter 16

THE WELCOME MAT

What greater thing is there for two human souls
than to feel that they are joined to strengthen
each other and to be at one with each other
in silent unspeakable memories.
—George Eliot

The feelings of ease and fit continued as I introduced Will to those around me. As I explained already, he embraced my kids as soon as he met them and vice versa—something that I think is essential in a second marriage. I never could have opened my heart and my life to anyone who was not open to my kids, challenges and all, and we had plenty of those bringing together three teenagers and a middle schooler.

We were super careful about integrating the kids and took a bit of time to do that. After a few months, we decided to try it over sushi and hoped for the best. Sushi does seem to help most situations. I would never say it was easy, and the kids often expressed the challenge of trying to support the process, but we eventually became our own family. Some of my best memories are of the six of us traveling together, most recently to Italy where despite a lost bag and eventually COVID in Venice, we ate, we drank, and we saw some of the most amazing sights. I am not sure I have ever laughed harder than playing Cards Against Humanity sitting on our balcony in our Punta Mita rental. Even some of our 2020 pandemic times were full of joyful and silly moments.

I recognize that we are lucky and that there are plenty of second marriages in which the kids do not click this way or accept the new wife or husband or partner even though the love connection may otherwise feel like a fit. I just know that for me, I needed this relationship to work at all levels, from my Oliver on up. Of course, Oliver loved Will more than he did me after about three weeks. Zach pretty much glued himself to Will from day one, and Will has been an exceptional guiding force in his life at a time when it was critical. The important point is that fitting into your family can sometimes mean creating a new family that feels stronger and better.

The ease of the fit extended to all members of my family who could not be happier that I found a true equal who was going to support me. There were many things about Will that reminded me of my dad—his calm disposition, his dry sense of humor, and weirdly the way he greased down his hair. Will now has much cooler, ungreased hair— sorry, Dad. There was also a gentleness and kindness that drew me to Will; they reminded me of my dad and, thinking even farther back, of my grandpa Nate, who is a hero in my life.

It certainly is very different meeting someone so much later in life. I barely got to know Will's mother, whom I adored immediately, and who quickly learned that I was the ticket to updates on Will and the boys. By the time we met, Will's dad was diagnosed with Alzheimer's, and every time we went to visit him, he asked who I was. This made me feel both sad and detached, even though it clearly was not his fault or intent. Will was extremely patient and answered every question his father asked over and over again, and he introduced me each time. I feel a bit cheated out of getting to know my in-laws, but that was not in the cards for us. I do know that Will's mother explained on her death bed that she was so happy that he had found someone, and a nice Jewish girl at that. I also picked up another sister in the mix, and she and her husband have been yet another gift to my life and the life of my kids.

The friend part was not quite as easy for us, as Will is an introvert and is not a huge fan of chitchat. He is the kind of person who does amazing one-on-one, but superficial banter is not his forte. He loves having deeper conversations and really getting to know people. He tends to be a quiet listener, a quality I have tried to mirror and continue to admire. Thus, it takes a bit more of an effort to truly get to know him and to see the gem of a human and husband he is. I am so grateful for the friends who took the time to do that and to include him, making our new life a part of my old one.

One of my BFFs who lived through many of my horrible dates from afar insisted that she needed to provide her seal of approval before this so-called dating could continue. During a trip to the Big Apple, she interviewed Will over sushi (do you see a theme there?), only to proclaim that he reminded her of Don Draper. *Mad Men* is literally my favorite show, and she definitely meant the kind, sweet version of Don Draper. It was likely the greased-down hair. The good news is that she could not endorse him highly enough. While external validation is helpful, and I often wished people would have warned me more about my previous bad choices, I already knew in my heart by this time that Will was my person.

It was also interesting to get to know Will's high school friends since they are Will's main friend group. They text multiple times a day and have stayed in touch for many decades. I loved hearing about all the Grateful Dead concerts and Indiana University shenanigans. They were so kind and open to getting to know me during our first visit for the Indy 500, a staple in Will's previous life. I could actually feel their excitement about Will finding happiness. They live all over the country, though, so there are very few chances for all of us to further integrate and connect.

Family and friends make up so much of our history and are such important parts of our lives. When you are with the right person in a relationship, with someone who makes you feel confident, it is a gift to introduce him to your family and friends. I felt such a sense of pride when I showed up with Will for Rosh Hashanah at my aunt's or for a friend's birthday party or even at any type of work event, where I have a team I consider family as well. The two main guys on my team are probably two of the most important people in my life, and they bonded with Will incredibly quickly. In fact, the three of them have almost all the same interests and randomly look alike. Their stamp of approval meant quite a lot to me.

There is also the very extended network of friends on Facebook and Instagram, where story lines are borne through pictures and events that don't often align with reality. My kids are always talking about people's dating "becoming Insta-official," whatever that means. Will is not a social-media guy, but I will admit that it has been fulfilling to share with the world that I have found my happily ever after. As much as I have felt the support within my small inner circle, I often feel it in my broader connections also, where our only ongoing contacts may be a sporadic "like" or "love." The distinction that is important, though, is that you should never feel as if you have to show the world you are happy and in a good relationship if you are not. That serves no one. Digging deep enough to think about how and why you are posting is mission critical to evaluating your relationship and overall feeling of being in love.

At the end of the day, only your opinion matters, but I agree with the love stories that emphasized it is important to find a love that fits into your life at all levels. Being able to feel pride with your plus-one by your side in all your endeavors is confirmation of a fit that is sweeter and more meaningful because it can be shared with family and friends.

Chapter 17

THE VAULT

Find the person who will love you because of your differences and not in spite of them and you ave found a lover for life.
—Leo Buscaglia

As I was writing the second half of the book, I decided to perform a data-quality check post-pandemic to make sure that my fifteen-year-old data on relationships was still valid. (Chapter 18 provides a summary of that exercise.) As part of the process, one new theme emerged in these conversations that I coincidentally had already started to write about as part of my own two bonus themes. These conversations provided validation of my belief that feeling safe to share your deepest secrets with your significant other is a definitive sign that you have a foundation of true love. Both a forty-five-year-old lawyer and her adorable, very cool mom answered my question of how they knew they were in love in a way that referenced they both felt safe to share their deepest feelings and secrets. Thus, I am adding in the theme about creating this incredible safe space that infiltrates many of the love stories. While it may seem very similar to previous themes about comfort and feeling at home, it goes a bit deeper and is wider in its impact.

For me, this feeling of safety was the cornerstone of how I knew that Will was the person I needed to spend my life loving and why I had to make sure this theme was considered in my overall analysis. My belief is that feeling safe is essential to feeling happy. Part of the impact of this theme is that it promotes true authenticity, which I think is critical in every aspect of my life. If you are in "fake it until you make it" mode, you will exhaust yourself quickly.

There is a physical-safety component, for sure. Who does not prefer someone in the house with you when you hear some crazy noise in the middle of night and think someone is breaking in? Or for me, I feel safe when I lay my head on Will's chest and can hear him breathing. I am the person who does not sleep great when Will travels, and it's not because I am binge-watching the *Real Housewives of New York*. It is partly because Felix likes to go from his dog bed to our bed to his dog bed, rinse and repeat. It is mostly because I don't feel safe when Will is not around. I admit that last statement is very hard for this super-independent woman to say.

The ultimate test in the area of feeling safe, though, is if you can share your biggest fear or secret with your partner. If you feel as if you are safe to do that, then you have created a space in which you can be yourself. For me, the deepest secret that I had held very close to my vest was that I have alopecia. I have had hair loss and balding since puberty, and it has been an ongoing personal struggle and a huge source of embarrassment for me. After seeing many doctors and finally finding an incredible dermatologist at the Cleveland Clinic back in high school, we figured out that I have too much of one male hormone, and therefore male-pattern baldness. When my mom was pregnant with me, I measured very small, which would not surprise anyone since I am four feet eleven inches on a good day. As a result, her brilliant OB-GYN decided to give her male hormones with the hopes it would increase my growth. Well, I still came out unable to reach most kitchen cabinets, but with the added "benefit" of dealing with hair loss most of my life.

This is not something I share with the world lightly, and I would never be in a place to do it if it were not for Will. It is the number one thing that stressed me while dating, so if I am going to be authentic about my dating history, I need to share it. I have a brilliant hairdresser who has helped me "cover up" my issue on some level for years. At first, it was a combination of extensions and black eyeshadow on my head to cover the balding spots. Can you imagine how embarrassing it is when someone kisses your head and ends up with black dust on their face, or when after lying on a pillow, you leave some black eyeshadow behind? I only told one other person I dated about the issue and not even the full extent. I was convinced that no one wanted a balding forty-something anyway.

It's important to know that before the extensions and black makeup fix, I had seen many doctors and tried virtually everything. Throughout high school, I had cortisone shots in my head monthly, which included numerous small shots that were incredibly painful. I went on to try different medications, every version of Rogaine, and even had consults about hair transplants. My problem, though, is not very fixable at its source; thus, I have learned to both accept it and work around it while managing to be grateful that it is often the worst thing I have to deal with.

Think about what you focus on when you first see someone, especially a female. It is virtually always the hair. Or maybe the face and the boobs and then the hair. I have had hair envy ten ways to Tuesday for so many people whom I have encountered in my life. Scroll through Instagram—how many ads do you see for products related to your hair—straighten it, control volume, curl it, you name it? Hair is equivalent to beauty, and I was convinced that my lack of it put me at a deficit for life, especially in terms of finding anyone who would think I was attractive. A bald guy can be hot, but a girl with thin hair and bald spots? Not so much.

I wish I clearly remembered when I finally told Will about the alopecia and allowed him to see me when I looked my absolute worst—without the black eyeshadow after a shower. The thing is, I don't remember. While I know it was early on, he made it such a nonevent that I don't even recall it. It made me feel that he was able to see the real me, even with so much less hair than most, and love me for me and not for how I thought others defined me.

This is my baggage, and I carry it; sometimes it becomes heavy. As it gets worse, I always continue to worry that it will eventually bother Will. As I started menopause and had to embrace my ever-changing hormones and further loss of estrogen, my hair loss did get worse. I had to move to wearing wig toppers and eventually to partial wigs. It still makes me sad and gets me down on occasion, especially when I am out in a windstorm, holding my hair on and praying it does not fly off, or outside in crazy heat with a hairpiece that adds another twenty degrees to my current hot flashes. There is the bonus, though, that getting ready can be a breeze if you can just clip on your hair. What is not a breeze is figuring out how to do yoga without showing your baldness to the world, which is why I love my headscarves and am so grateful they are back in style. I never feel more loved than when I share these ongoing fears and challenges with Will, and he exudes so much empathy.

Yes, there is much worse stuff in life. Will and I had a good laugh when he went through chemo, and I shaved what hair he had left on his head; he had glorious hair. I told him we could now be twins. I was tempted to just shave my own head at that time and call it a day. Up until now, I have hidden this secret from most people, but we all have something that we think makes us unlovable. I compensated for years, making sure I was so thin and had other traits during my dating days to offset the one issue I hoped no one would notice, and I tried so hard to cover it up. Yet when Will came into my life, I was able to uncover it, share it, and feel supported in a way I had never felt. Hey, he even drops my hairpieces off to my fab hairdresser for styling. How's that for a devoted husband?

Will did not have any kind of similar secret he was trying to hide from the world or that made him feel heavy. Just a missing middle finger from some bad choices in Jamaica when he was twenty and a skinny calf from a ruptured Achilles tendon that a doctor weirdly advised him not to fix. He also now has an uneven chest from the mastectomy, but to me, these are what make him Will. These are the things that emulate strength and perseverance, two things that I love so much about him.

Hopefully, you do not have something that you pray no one will find out. If you do, I hope you find the person whom you can share it with, with no judgment and all love, so that you can be in a relationship that allows you to be your authentic self and "let your hair down."

Chapter 18

PERFECT HARMONY

In dreams and in love there are no impossibilities.
—Janos Arany

I was a bit surprised that the love stories I heard many years ago did not include more about goals, objectives, and dreams. Instead, they were more about feelings, connections, and fit. My own observation is that two people need to be going in the same direction in order to be able to support each other while getting there. That direction may take a turn here and there that will require some bobbing and weaving, but you really need to want the same things. Thus, my final theme to add into the mix is a general alignment of goals and objectives. A theme that I personally identify as essential, but one my love targets did not really emphasize.

I certainly do not mean alignment of all the same things. Will claims he wants to open a tiki bar one day on a beach in Mexico. Not sure I am embracing that, but I would be happy to run a small yoga studio as long as our condo has a view of the ocean. I definitely don't mean aligning the small things like TV shows, movies, or even music, although some common ground can be helpful. Instead, I am referring to the big stuff.

Where do you want live? Do you like to travel? What kind of work mandates do you have, and how do these impact your relationship? When do you want to retire? What kinds of colleges do you want your kids to attend? What are your views on supporting the kids postcollege. (I highly encourage everyone to discuss this one up front—adulting is a slow roll these days). These are just a few examples and may not be things most couples talk about, especially when they are young and considering marriage for the first time.

This does not mean that compromise is not essential to the long-term happiness of couples. I have become better at reaching compromises in life and in work. It may seem impossible to think about where you want to be in twenty years and to talk about those things up front. Sure, some of it is impossible to know with certainty because we cannot predict what will happen. If Will did not get breast cancer, we may never have doubled down on Cleveland because of its health care and bought what would be our dream house in Cleveland Heights. While we regularly discussed where we wanted to live in the future, we never really knew that home base may remain here for us.

It is easier to tell if your morals, values, and overall life objectives align. The "kids versus no kids" or "how many kids" decision is an easy one and certainly a foundational discussion. More generally, how you want to live your personal and professional lives, how you see those kids being raised, and what role you may want to take in your community are all essential baseline convos that should not be avoided.

I expected to hear a bit more, from those I chatted with, that their dreams aligned from the beginning or their dreams continued to align over time, but interestingly the topic did not come up, or at least I did not have it in my notes. It is possible that people considering a post-kid second marriage may focus more on this topic than two thirty-year-olds approaching a first marriage, but even those whom I interviewed who were giving marriage a second go-around did not talk about dream alignment as a fundamental concept. If nothing else, considering these various topics will force you to think about your own dreams and goals in a way you have not done before.

Part of the reason that I had to include dream alignment as a theme is because it has been the cornerstone of so many conversations I have had with women as they are separating from their husbands. Those conversations have been filled with dream misalignment and moral conflicts. There have been many discussions about how "we just do not want the same things" or "he does not support my professional goals" or even worse, "we just cannot agree on parenting." I often pried and asked if they had spoken about these things at the beginning of their relationship, when they first came together, but sadly the answer was usually no or "I don't remember." I realize I was asking a very difficult question at a time of extreme trauma. These conversations echoed in my head every time I went on a date, and I was convinced that I had to have candid and important discussions of what I wanted in my life, my kids' lives, and my future up front.

While we are almost ten years apart and grew up in slightly different generations, Will and I were raised with very similar morals and values. I am blessed by the fact that he had a strong mother who taught him that strong women are to be admired and respected. Will is always one to brainstorm my career goals and ideas, and no one supports those goals more than he. I try to always be his biggest cheerleader in supporting what his next chapters may look like, and these were concepts that we talked about from day one. We also quickly learned that we viewed family, parenting, and the importance of community involvement the same way. I already shared our alignment on parenting, which actually allowed me to grow in all new ways and improve the way I thought about and addressed motherhood.

I am not delusional in thinking that we all know where we want to go in life when we are looking for our significant other, especially those savvy enough to find their person on the first try. What I do believe is that if you find someone with similar morals, values, and goals, and you both view the world through a similar lens, then you can support each other's dreams and end up in a relationship that is both fulfilling and exciting. You may even end up at a tiki bar, drinking a margarita on a beach with the love of your life.

Chapter 19

ENDURING HEARTS

It is love that asks, that seeks, that knocks,
that finds, and that is faithful to what it finds.
—St. Augustine

I opted not to continue my research after I wrote part I of
the book and never picked it up again until recently
since I found my own answers. Yet, like any good attorney,
I felt I had to spot-check my conclusions to make sure
they survived the test of time. This quality-control check
only included talking to a handful of new people. People
whom I view as having loving relationships, but people
who were not in my life during my initial search for love
stories but are a large part of my life now.

The one theme that continued to be ever present during
these more recent discussions was the easy-peasy piece.
Everyone I spoke to mentioned how easy meeting their
spouse or significant other was and how much like home it
felt. A new dear neighborhood friend who is only slightly

older than I retold a story about meeting her husband at a time when she was considering moving to Montana as part of her higher-education experience, a location most people did not embrace. After being reluctantly dragged to a party to get fixed up with someone else, she instead met her now husband after he sat next to her on a sofa, only to later explain that he had just moved back to Cleveland from Montana. This love story also further validated my belief that there definitely is a bit of luck and karma in the process.

What is even crazier about that couple who have been married for over three decades is that they have recently gone through the worst thing a parent can ever experience, the loss of a child. Yet, somehow, these two have managed to become closer than ever, giving each other space to grieve. The theme about riding waves was echoed, as they have taken turns pulling each other up during this long, horrific process. Some of the other themes came to the forefront during our chat as well, including how well he fit in with her family and friends and the whole concept of how he felt like home. Plus, he does everything she hates to do, like cook.

A trainer who has been married for forty-one years also had a story of luck and coincidence. She met her husband while she was on a trip to Florida. He was from a super-small town in the middle of nowhere, but, coincidentally, it is the exact same small town where her grandmother was born. In addition to this kismet, she explained quite a bit about fit and ease. She emphasized how he makes her a better person and that one of the reasons she loves him so much after all these years is that he is such a great father and grandfather.

Not being able to imagine life without his partner was a strong theme my Pilates instructor shared with me. They have been together for over twenty years. They met online originally, shortly after he came to the United States. While he explained that he first knew his partner was the one after they had sex, he also described the ease of their discussions and interactions, even with a language barrier back then, which really says something.

While my younger, fun attorney friend enjoyed answering the "when" question, her focus was much more on the new theme that evolved—feeling safe and comfortable enough to be "totally myself." While she was dating someone else when she met her husband, the connection and ease that was created after they met made it very clear to her how wrong for her that old relationship was. This new love story also provided validation of the theme about focusing on sex and physical connection as well as the ability to share things that she might be embarrassed or hesitant to tell others. "He just makes the shitty parts of life so much better," my younger friend explained. She also confirmed that he makes her want to be her best self at all times— checking that theme off as well. While I have had the joy of counseling them through a few tiny tiffs, I know neither of them can see life without the other.

The shared burden in riding the waves was front and center in all these new discussions and was one of the reasons each of these new subjects felt that their relationship had endured the test of time. It was probably the most universal theme I heard this time around, aside from the overall priority of ease.

I felt as if I could continue my research forever because it brings me so much joy to see someone's face light up when talking about the love of their life. Taking the time to remember where it all started serves us all well. In fact, every year on our anniversary, Will and I read our wedding vows to each other. This is part of our overall commitment to each other, but also an important reminder of the impactful words we crafted for the day we had both waited a lifetime to reach.

After completing my 2024 data update, I felt confident that the themes that shone through all the love stories so many years ago are still relevant and viable today. Every person has a twist on each of the themes and a unique experience, yet these themes remind us that there are unifying concepts that are central to finding the person who is right for you. The person who fits into your world in a way that can provide a happily ever after.

Part III

LOVE LESSONS LEARNED

3LS ON THE ROAD TO TRUE LOVE

After reflecting back on my interviews and my own journey, a variety of love lessons surfaced, which I have aptly named 3Ls (bad lawyer joke—no, not third-year law students). My goal in developing the 3Ls is to support others as they attempt to find true love while hopefully avoiding some of the pitfalls, mistakes, and endless thoughts that trapped my heart and my mind. There were so many things I learned through my almost ten-year process that I wish someone had shared with me so that I would have been able to minimize some of the heartache and tears that I experienced. While I realize that every person is on their own journey and has their own process, I hope that I can help just one person change her mindset and find her true love; then we will have two more happy hearts in this world. Another lid that fits a pot! Plus, after 104 dates, an unsuccessful marriage, and hearing so many beautiful love stories, I must have learned something.

LLL Number 1

PUT YOURSELF OUT THERE

The smile is the beginning of love.
—**Mother Teresa**

I tend to be "that friend" who asks every single or divorced person if they are actively dating. In fact, if I meet you at a cocktail party and learn you are single, I may ask you those very questions, even if I hardly know you. I run through the usual gamut of inquiries related to divorce and dating, but I always ask if the person has tried online dating. The responses are mixed, as you can imagine, but I cannot tell you how many people are closed off to the idea. While I did not meet the love of my life on an app or a website, it serves an amazing purpose. Plus, I do know some people who had success finding true love online, including my old au pair, so you never know.

Similar to interviewing for a job, with dating you need experience. Thus, I always recommend trying online dating just to put yourself "out there," wherever your "out there" may be at the time. I remember so clearly when I first decided that I would put a profile on Match.com. I remotely remember my profile name was something like yogamom11, or maybe a username that is even lamer than that. One of my gal pals came over, and we did a photoshoot in my living room. I wore a black tank and tan duster. Some pics with the duster and some without. This was back in the day when I was borderline starving myself for fear of being naked in front of someone new, so I was pleased to show my arms and tried desperately to look as if I had good hair.

What a balancing act putting a profile together was then, and I imagine still is now. This is where my life motto of "All truth, all the time" goes out the window. My tagline could not be "Single Mom of Two Who Enjoys Red Wine and *Downton Abbey*" or "While I Am Barely Five Feet, I Love *People* Magazine and Hosting Dance Parties with My Kids." You have to be cute and flirty, but not too cute and flirty. You need to be interesting, but not so interesting that someone feels intimidated. You have to be out there, but not too aggressive. You have to look successful so you don't look needy, but not too successful. You need to sound fun and fabulous even if you feel sad and boring. And of course, whatever you do, do not post a picture with your kids if you are a single mom. Bonus points if you include a kid pic, though, if you are a single dad. In fact,

I cannot tell you how many guys apparently borrowed kids for pictures back then.

I remember showing up for a date at a wine bar in Chagrin Falls. It was a Match.com connection that I had vetted pretty thoroughly—meaning many emails back and forth and an internet search to make sure he was not a serial killer or in bankruptcy (I had one of those— someone in bankruptcy, but not a serial killer, at least not that I know of). I was mildly excited leading up to our first in-person meetup, as there was a supercute picture of him with two adorable kids. Turns out those adorable kiddos were his niece and nephew, and he enjoyed his playdates with kids but was "not a fan of kids" generally. Talk about a bait and switch.

Then there were guys who were so fit they felt they needed to include a shirtless photo so all the Match.com users would have proof, or those guys who elected to post their college-graduation photo even though its twenty years old. I even received a few dick pics in my messages, but that was an easy, hard no (pun intended). I was always put off by the guys who wrote superlong bios, dismissing them as trying too hard. So while I was struggling with my own profile, I definitely examined every profile of a potential date as if it were the most important legal brief I ever had to redline.

As part of the profile process, you have to pick various options for your target date—parameters such as age range, height, and interests. I am a huge fan of online shopping. In fact, Will thinks the UPS guy is going to worry if a day goes by in which nothing is delivered. Yet my ability to pick these factors, at first, put too many rules in my head. Initially, I looked way too narrowly when I selected my options. Instead, I suggest casting the net as wide as your mind can tolerate in terms of distance as well as age, interests, and professions. The most successful relationship I had during my almost ten years of single days, which I mentioned at the beginning of the book, was from Match.com with a guy whom I would have never met otherwise. The relationship ended up serving as really good practice. As I tell my kids, even when a relationship does not work, you need to stop and figure out what you learned from it.

I am not even sure what apps other than Tinder and Bumble are out there these days. I know many thirtysomethings in big cities seem to rely on apps as the only way to meet someone. As I explain in a subsequent LLL, I would not rely solely on technology, but I would embrace the concept that dating apps are the perfect way to put yourself out there at your own pace to meet someone whom you would have never met.

Relying on apps or dating websites is also not the only way to get "out there." I have heard such fun stories about running groups, hiking clubs, clay classes, yoga, and more. Joining something new brings a mix of people into your circle whom you would have never met otherwise. And these new people have single friends, which even further expands your potential circle of target fix-ups. What I can assure you is the chance of meeting your person while sitting at home in your PJs and scrolling Instagram reels is very low.

Facebook is not all bad in the world of dating. Leveraging Facebook can even be a semi-safe way to put yourself out there. I created my Facebook profile around the same time I started online dating. I remember that picture vividly; it did include my two kiddos. I was wearing a black halter top, again trying to look cute but natural. This was a picture that I took for the initial posting, but only after I inspected virtually every other picture I already had with my kids and decided they did not provide the right vibe—and yes, I embrace the insanity of that exercise. As soon as my Facebook profile was set up, I spent an inordinate amount of time looking up the status of old boyfriends. While I generally do not advocate looking backwards, one of my dearest and oldest friends at my law firm had a terrible divorce, reconnected with a high school boyfriend on Facebook, who she still felt was the love of her life, and now they are married and living happily together in Connecticut.

While there are certain positives to it, I am still not the hugest fan of social media overall because I believe that spending too much time focusing on others just increases your loneliness and longing during a time when you are trying to find a partner. Keep in mind that "comparison is the thief of joy" (Theodore Roosevelt). While I introduced myself to Facebook at the same time I doubled down on dating, I shed many tears seeing so many happy families together, which I longed so desperately to have and felt guilty for not providing to my kids. There is a yin and a yang to it, and I want to be transparent that scrolling does not often bring joy. What I do not recommend is friending the people you date on Facebook or Instagram. While it can certainly help you with due diligence, things can quickly get awkward if the dates do not go well, although maybe that is what they made unfriending for.

These are just a few ideas of how you can open your heart and mind in the dating world. Mixing my dating horror stories with my LLL to put yourself out there may seem contradictory, but I do think that every bad, failed, and pitiful date allowed me to grow as a person. Each of these connections became part of my travels through a process that allowed me to figure out what I really wanted and needed in a partner.

At the risk of sounding like a crazy Jewish mother, my disclaimer is to make sure to use the apps wisely, which requires time, thought, and a very careful vetting process. Of course, always tell a friend where you are going, and pick a safe, busy public place. Always have an escape vehicle and an exit strategy, which hopefully you will not have to use. Most importantly, have low expectations. Consider it a practice round, and you might be surprised.

LLL Number 2

THE LUCK OF LOVE

This fire that we call loving is too strong for human minds. But just right for human souls.
—**Aberjhani**

I believe in karma. Karma is one of the reasons I always want to do for others as I would want done for me if I needed help, support, or kindness. I have personally seen some karmic universal shifts in which people have finally received what they deserve (at least in my opinion), which is sometimes not the best of things. Perhaps it's my obsession with yoga and meditation or my general belief that the world should be fair. Either way, when it comes to dating and finding the one, I believe there is both timing and luck involved.

Will and I always talk about the fact that if the real estate market had not crashed and he had not lost his job in Indiana, he would not have dragged his middle school kids to Cleveland, Ohio, to become CEO of the port here.

Then he would have never encountered Ann, and we would never have met and ended up together. So what seemed like the worst luck at the time is now the best luck possible for both of us.

Meeting your match is about timing as well. Will separated from his ex-wife shortly after moving to Cleveland and at a time when I had dated around enough that I had eroded all my dating rules. I can honestly say that if Ann had told me about Will when I first got divorced, I am not sure whether I would have been open to dating someone nine and a half years older—how dumb would that have been? It really does have to be the right place and the right time.

One of my favorite stories about our luck and timing, which is also a story about our busy lives, is that Will and I both ended up in the same airport on the same connecting flight home a few years ago without knowing it. After that, we decided that we really should do a better job at exchanging our travel information. We asked the kind person in the middle seat next to me to switch so we could sit together. It was truly one of those "you can't make this up" moments that was such a bright light at such a super-busy time. While I recognize that this silly story does not directly relate to finding a match, I think it highlights that at certain times the universe, or at least United Airlines, just puts people together.

Lots of the stories that I was told during my interviews included tales of timing and luck that had brought these people together. How about that story about my neighbor and Montana? Nana's story included the fact that her second husband got divorced shortly after she did, and she had never stopped thinking about him, even though their timing had not worked the first time. My younger lawyer pal only met her husband after she was dragged out to a bar by her roommate after spending the day crying since her current boyfriend had not treated her well. So what would life be like if she had never gone to that bar? These are the kinds of questions that blow my mind and remind me that there is an element of timing to each of these connections. People come together in all kinds of crazy ways, but I will always believe that luck plays a role in the elusive concept of love.

How do you embrace this LLL though? Well, you give a bit of the process up to the universe and have some faith. Maybe it's more of an observation than an LLL, but the observation is a reminder that luck and timing do not often find you at your house on your sofa. If you follow LLL number one and put yourself out there, luck and timing will do their thing when the time is right for it to happen. While we all have some control over the outcome by participating and being willing to make connections, at the end of the day, true love will appear when it is meant to be—a perfect combination of action and inaction.

LLL Number 3

NO PROJECTS

*The greatest happiness in life is the conviction
that we are loved; loved for ourselves, or rather,
loved in spite of ourselves.*
—Victor Hugo

One of my favorite sayings is "You do you." I really began to embrace this mantra on my fiftieth birthday. While I struggled at times to do me personally and socially, I did not have the same struggle of embracing my wants and needs in my career. When it comes to being a lawyer, I have always been 100 percent committed to paving the way for other women by creating a path that worked for me and my life as mostly a single mom who also very much cared about her clients and career in addition to her children.

Inspired by the You Do You concept, I wrote a *Bloomberg* article for my milestone birthday, which also happened to be the twenty-fifth year of my law practice. The main point of the article was a summary of what I wish I had known when I was twenty-five and starting my legal practice with the mantra that you do not have to be just like anyone else to succeed. Portions of this book are a twist on that article, as I share what I wish I had known when I was dating and looking for a partner back when I was twenty-five. Rule number one back then would have been to focus on being your authentic self and making sure that your plan is not to change someone else. Authenticity is the foundation for a great relationship. So not only do you need to accept yourself, but your partner also has to accept you fully and completely.

Like everyone, I have changed and grown over the years. As you get older, your priorities shift, and you tend to care less about certain things. While more people might annoy you, you also learn to make decisions that make you happy and build boundaries that allow you to create spaces that generate peace. So when I say that you should not have to change for a relationship, I am not advocating that people do not change or that people should not set goals or aim to erase bad habits or practices. Individuals certainly grow and mature and figure things out. They work through past traumas so that they can have an open heart and be their best self for a relationship. They stop drinking. They go back to school. They seek therapy. All these types of changes are constructive and helpful for your own life and that of those around you.

What I am saying is that you should not have to change your goals in life or your personality for someone else. I had a friend whose husband told her she talked too much and another friend whose spouse complained that she was too career oriented. These are parts of you that the right person should embrace and support. From a female perspective, we know it is hard for men to feel complete with a wife or girlfriend who may make more money than they do or have more career success, but it has been such a gift to see some of my female partners with spouses who agreed to stay home and raise kids so she can work and achieve the success she envisioned.

The flip side is that you cannot plan to change someone else. Yes, you can plan to make sure those boat shoes go missing or the wide-brimmed hat that looks ridiculous ends up in the Goodwill pile. But it is not our job to change someone. Plus, spoiler alert—it does not work. As I explained earlier, I have always lived like Olivia Pope, both in life and work, with the objective that I could fix just about every problem. My massage professional needs legal help; let me give you some advice. My client needs a divorce lawyer; I will find the perfect one. When any of our four kids have a problem, I tend to jump in way too soon. Something I regret now, because learning how to fix things yourself is one of the most important skills in life.

So I am an admitted serial over-fixer. The place I exercised this most was in my PW (pre-Will) dating life with basically every date I ever went on from college through my marriage and the 103 dates after that. While this theme certainly tags along with the Don't Settle LLL (see below), it runs deeper because I have had way too many conversations with women heading for divorce that focused on her failure to be able to change her spouse after, initially, she thought that her significant other would become more motivated, more supportive, a better father, and sometimes even less abusive. There may be times when the one who needs some changing agrees to try to change, but in many cases, the issues tend to be a fundamental component of that person's being. While the traits may hide for a while, they will come back, and it's not our job to modify those traits or make someone become something they are not. It's exhausting, not very rewarding, and just makes you feel defeated and depleted.

When Nana conveyed her love story to me, she advised me to think about the guy I was dating at the time and identify the trait I liked the least about him. She explained that, whatever trait came to mind, this same trait will just get bigger and worse over time, even if it seemed cute at the moment. Thus, you need to dig deep to see if this trait will get in the way of your happiness and ability to feel complete in the Jerry Maguire kind of way. I am not talking about issues like snoring (I highly recommend a sound machine); instead, I am referring to a person's fundamental personality traits.

I can honestly say, when I put Will to Nana's test many years back, there was not a single trait that I could think of that I did not like. In fact, he had so many positive traits that I never thought I would see in a partner and several of which I aimed to achieve on my journey to growth and learning. The core of who he is includes every quality I admire in people and some that I see in very few.

Once I was able to turn off the voice in my head that used to tell me that "he will change" or "I can fix this," I was so much freer to look for a love that was perfect just as he was, rather than trying to become someone or something else. While I still may have to pretend on occasion to enjoy listening to the *Goose* or hiking, I am my authentic self with my partner, and I did not go into the relationship thinking I could change anything about him or that I needed to change anything about myself. I was able to fully embrace the You Do You as I did me in the most authentic way possible.

LLL Number 4

SHOUT IT FROM THE ROOFTOPS

Love is the ultimate truth at the heart of the universe and transcends all boundaries.
—Deepak Chopra

As a supplement to my LLL that you have to put yourself out there, I will add that putting yourself out there means telling people you want to meet someone. I don't mean telling your besties or even those whom you interact with regularly, who likely already know about your quest. Instead, it is all about informing people you may not know well to access untapped circles of options.

This is not only how I found love, but how several others I know have found love. I am constantly trying to fix people up to pay back the world for bringing me Will. Ideally, you are asking thoughtful people if they know anyone. Be aware that once you ask, you will likely receive the age-old response, "Tell me what you are looking for." My suggestion is to be as open as possible, but, of course, there may be some boundaries for certain daters. Someone with kids may be a no-go or perhaps he has to live close to you. Overall, remember to cast that net wide.

I also find that people generally want to help, and they love being asked if they know anyone for a fix-up. It may feel slightly awkward at first, but I suggest looking at it as part of your journey. The chance of Will and me crossing orbits without the help of Ann was pretty slim, although I often wonder if I would have met him eventually. When I think about this process, I have a visual of many small circles all intertwined, and the more you reach out and ask, the broader the diagram looks for you to reach the one you are meant to be with at this time in your life (that is, the number of circles gets bigger and wider).

I recognize that many do not want to mix work with dating; therefore, asking colleagues may be off-limits. I once spent many months convincing a work bestie to date a law partner of ours who had been pursuing her for quite a while. She lived by the golden rule that dating and work do not mix, but something told me that this was also a rule to be broken in this case. They indeed got married. The funniest part of the story is that, the day of their wedding, the firm intranet crashed because so many people were looking up her new husband's bio since she held a higher profile job in the firm, and he was not nearly as well known. In the end, the fact that they were together is all that matters. And remember, you can always find a new job.

So it's time to ask those in CrossFit or book club or that friend of a friend at a cocktail party. When someone asks me if I know anyone, I always appreciate the confidence, and my helper instincts kick in. I then make it my personal mission to find them a potential match. While I agree that sometimes love just finds you, telling the world you are looking is a great first step.

LLL Number 5

TUNING IN TO LOVE

Love is divine only and difficult always.
—**Toni Morrison**

As someone who talks a lot, I have a personal aspiration to learn to listen more and speak less. Will would tell you that I should keep trying, but it really is important while you are dating. First, because people love to talk about themselves. This will allow you to learn a ton about your date. One of my tests in determining the success of a date is whether and how much my date inquired about me, my kids, or my life. I don't mean the silly feigned interest— "Tell me about yourself?" I mean real questions. Without those, he is not worth a second date. I went on too many dates where, believe it or not, I did not say virtually anything, other than asking the guy questions about himself and his life. Several of the guys seemed to be thrilled to just drone on and on about themselves. It was during these painful interactions back then that I needed the earplugs I use every night now to tune out Will's snoring.

Listening closely to these initial conversations will usually provide various nuggets of insight into the person you are sipping wine with or sharing a platter of hummus and veggies. The guy whom I was dating initially after my divorce, the one who told me that he was divorced but actually was not, slipped up during a conversation. I am grateful I was listening closely. Plus, waiting to hear his interest in you signals so much about whether this connection may be a go or a no-go.

The other thing about listening is gauging how you feel with this person in silence. Sure, at first, silence is usually awkward. In fact, I am constantly finding myself trying to fill the void in every situation with random small talk. Yet being able to sit in silence with someone and feel calm is a true gift. It means you have a comfort with the presence of the other person that goes beyond words. This goes back to the first trip to Columbus that I took with Will. This was when I embraced the fact that we could sit in silence without it feeling awkward, a gift I had been waiting for my entire life.

The other part of the listening rule is about listening to your gut. This is a rule that I have broken too many times to count. I think my gut did not know how to speak up during the first thirty-five years of my life. Thank goodness it eventually found its voice, but I have to listen very intently still to hear it. I do believe your gut centers you and will tell you if something is right or wrong generally in life, which includes dating. My gut told me when it was time to end my marriage, even though my heart hurt so badly for my children, and I did feel love for their father. My gut told me not to switch law firms a while back when I was feeling unappreciated for a short time after I failed to follow my own advice to speak up and ask for what I wanted. Every time I have listened to my gut, I have gone in the right direction.

I have a journal entry from July 9, 2009, that reflects my struggle with listening to my own wants and needs:

> *Why can I not be happy with myself and my life? I have a good life, but I would be lying if I did not acknowledge that there is a hole—something still missing. My lack of belief in myself on the right way to fill that hole is also a bit crazy. Do I have any judgment? Do I even know what is right for me? Am I telling myself what I want to hear rather than the truth? My saying stamped on my tea bag tonight said, "The Truth Is in You." It must be in here somewhere, right?*

I went on to write in that same entry:

> *I guess at the end of the day there is no denying that…I want to know that I can make a good, right choice, be in love and make it last and work. I want personal success in addition to professional success. But I need and want the right person standing next to me. Please give me the strength to slow it down and figure it out and know where to go on this path forward.*

I clearly recognized that my gut was not tuned up to where it needed to be back then because in a later entry, in August 2010, I go on to say:

[My neighbor] says to trust my little voice, but sometimes I think mine is broken.

Over time and with experience, my gut and little voice started to step up to the plate and sharpen in a way that I was able to build confidence in my choices and in my ability to know what would be good for me and my kids.

There were many times during my dating chaos that my gut told me not to go on a second or third date because this person was not the one, but I may have gone for practice or because I was bored or lonely. What I can say is that, the day that Will asked me to marry him, my gut was singing yes. The whole night was sort of hilarious. We were in Indy at a wedding of a high school friend of Will's and were heading into a bar to grab a drink before the rehearsal dinner. We pull up to the valet, and Will brings his briefcase into the restaurant. The ring was in there, as you might have guessed (and, clearly, he was afraid to leave it in the car), but he was acting so weird that I did get suspicious. There was no over-the-top proposal. The big event occurred while we were just sitting next to each other in our hotel room later that night, saying all the things I waited forty-three years to hear. It was perfect.

My gut felt the same way during our engagement even though it included selling the home my kids grew up in, which made me incredibly sad, and stressfully finding a house to live in that would bring our four kids together in a positive way. My gut continued to sing on our wedding day when I can honestly say I did not have a single doubt that becoming Heidi Friedman (I like to take on a new Jewish last name every so often) was my destiny and what I had waited for my whole life.

I used to make fun of those sayings "Trust your gut" or "What does your gut say?" But now I get it. My gut is louder and clearer than ever before. I know some of that comes with age, but it also comes with experience. This includes dating experience, knowing when it's time to start a relationship or end one. So listen closely to all of it, and you will hear so much wisdom.

LLL Number 6

THIS ISN'T A PLAYDATE

Love is the whole thing. We are only pieces.
—Rumi

I recognize that this LLL may be a bit controversial and borderline preachy, but I had to include it because I feel so strongly about it. If you don't have kids, you can skip this part! I don't mean adult kids who are grown and likely trying to set you up themselves. I mean younger kids who are very much part of your life equation but likely do not need the highs and lows of dating in their life.

I am very proud of the fact that I did not introduce my kids to anyone before Will. They were very young when I started the process of looking for my do-over, but certainly were old enough to understand. Every divorced family is different. I think it is wonderful if the exes get along great, share duties, and continue to love their kids unconditionally jointly, but there are also many situations in which one or the other starts dating someone new, quickly introduces that person to the kids, and it causes many rifts throughout the family.

I am not taking full credit for my decision, as I had a wonderful therapist throughout the process who was very much an advocate for the motto Your Kids Are Not Dating. She and I both had seen many broken hearts when moms or dads started dating someone who welcomed the child into their life only for the breakup to happen quickly while the kids are still trying to process the fact that their own parents have broken up.

I recognize that following this rule may be very complex logistically for many people, especially a single parent with sole custody. I was privileged to have the ability to have an au pair who was my lifesaver. Friends and family can hopefully help provide some time to get out there as well. This also means that visitors may only be welcome when the kids are not there or may be sleeping at grandma's house. The limitation on access provided a slowness to the pace of dating that I needed at the time. I would always feel guilty if I did sleep out, and the kids were at home with my au pair. But Mama's gotta have some fun!

My oldest was like an investigative reporter when I returned home after a night out, but as far as they knew, I was always out with friends. My kids were very much a topic of discussion during my dating years. If someone was not open to my kids and their challenges, then their reluctance made my decision easy. Virtually every guy I dated, except maybe a handful, were fathers themselves. I was the recipient of all kinds of unsolicited advice during that time—find someone with no kids, find someone who has older kids, don't date anyone with more than two kids, etc. Needless to say, this advice was not helpful. It was helpful to see what kind of a father my date might be, which I was usually able to figure out fairly quickly, especially for the ones who discussed being committed to baseball games, custody schedules, and homework. I was always open to taking on bonus kids, as I felt from date number one that only a father would understand my challenges as a mother and would allow us to support each other the way I needed to be supported. This proved to be true.

Dating has been analogized to a roller coaster, and I hate roller coasters. Remember, I am risk averse. But I can relate—the stomach drops the first time you meet someone or when he says he is not interested, but you think you might be. The high you feel when you get the text you have been waiting for or when someone winks back. Kids need stability, not roller coasters, and as much as life itself has its ups and downs, I have always felt that my job was to make their lives a bit more even-keeled and stable.

I already admitted the speed at which I introduced the kids to Will. He came to a family picnic at my house, as I figured I could use my parents and the others as buffers, or maybe it was just trial by fire. Will handled it beautifully and demonstrated a genuine interest in my parents and my kids. A month or so after that, he started sleeping over quite often. My youngest would come down in grey sweatpants and a T-shirt to match Will—he was attached to Will like Velcro. While Will certainly has magnetic qualities, it validated my gut feeling that I likely saved many broken hearts by waiting until their stepfather came into the picture before I merged my dating life with my family life.

The rules get a lot less clear when the relationship involves multiple sets of kids and bringing families together. As I explained earlier, we waited a bit before we tried to integrate the kids. No matter how great your kids are, I cannot imagine how weird meeting their mom's or dad's significant other must be for them. My only LLL around this is Don't Force It. Someone who had a successful second marriage with kids told me many years ago that it takes an average of seven years for combined families to fully be integrated and feel peaceful. I am pleased that we are above average, but I also know of too many awful stories in which things did not end up so kumbaya.

My bonus kids have added so much to my life. I have a new appreciation for music and the outdoors, as well as *Family Guy*. Plus, my bonus kids have added so much to the lives of my own kids, especially my youngest. The bond between these boys is something that I would have never dreamt could happen. My love for the two whom I did not birth is beyond anything I could have imagined. One of the most meaningful things to happen to me was when Will's ex-wife thanked me at the oldest' s graduation from college for the role that I played as a bonus mom to him in his life. I will say it again for those in the back—you can never have enough people who love and support you.

My life and the life of my two original kids has grown and expanded so much as our family got larger. Trying to get four young adults to truly "adult" at the same time is next level, but overall these new relationships impacted all of us in a positive way, making our lives so much more complete. True integration includes being open to every aspect of your partner's life, and what do we hold dearer than our children? My heart is so much fuller for loving all four of our kids.

Every situation is truly different, and I recognize that this book is not about integrating kids after a second marriage. I can only say that the kids add complexity to even the most perfect connection, and oftentimes quite a bit of extra stress. There is the extra challenge of trying to juggle your kid priorities without neglecting yourself and your own needs. Putting the kids first at every stage of the process can be a hefty burden, but when the right connection is made, integration can make everyone's life so much happier as long as there is patience, strategic timing, and a whole lotta love.

LLL Number 7

LOVE IS REALLY LOVE

Love conquers all things, so we too shall yield to love.
—**Virgil**

I would be remiss if I did not share an LLL I learned that was not entirely related to my research and my own dating life. That lesson is that love is really love, rainbows and all. I did interview several individuals who identify as queer as part of my original analysis, as well as my follow-up quality-control experiment, and their themes fell right in line with those couples in heteronormative relationships.

I have, however, developed a new level of appreciation for the sentiment that love is love, thanks to my oldest child. Born female, my oldest has gone through a true transition. Starting junior year of high school, she (at the time) announced that she was bisexual and spent some time dating women. Since then, veering toward identifying as lesbian and using the term *queer*, my kid has been in several long-term, same-sex relationships.

Most recently, the gender-identity piece has also transitioned. After identifying for a bit as *they/them*, there has been more of a transition to *he/they*, with some physical changes made as well. Morgan also seems to have an openness to date anyone that he/they feel connected to and to whom there is the potential for a relationship that will add to Morgan's life. Morgan is looking for the same love I was looking for, but has a wider, different lens in that search. I have seen with my own eyes that love is no less intimate or special if it is love between two women, two men, two transgender individuals, or some other combination. It can also be just as disappointing and hurtful if the relationship is not right.

It, however, can be more complicated. The hate in the world these days scares me, and we never want life to be harder for our kids, but I could not be prouder that Morgan is living an authentic life and learning to follow my LLL that dictates not changing for someone else. Maybe my next book will share my journey in parenting a child during this process and the mix of emotions and fears I have experienced. My job is to love and support my child, and I feel just as strongly that my oldest should not settle as they have done in the past and, instead, should find true love, no matter what he/she/they look like or identifies as in this world.

Firsthand, I have seen the judgment that is not all rainbows and balloons. What I say to people is to picture your child as the one who is queer and/or transitioning. Picture your child in a same-sex relationship but still so badly needing and wanting your love and support. There is no reason why we should love our offspring any less for the mere fact that they may love someone whom we did not anticipate or who may not fit our plan for them. This is the same reason we have no business judging who loves whom. What if this child were your child or your sister or your grandson? Mother Teresa's quote helped me articulate my role as a mother in this situation:

> *You will teach them to fly, but they will not fly your flight.*
>
> *You will teach them to dream, but they will not dream your dream.*
>
> *You will teach them to live, but they will not live your life.*
>
> *Nevertheless, in every flight, in every life, in every dream, the print of the way you taught them will remain.*

The themes and lessons I discovered on my journey are applicable to everyone. Just as love is universal, albeit intangible and difficult to find, the concept of love is just as difficult to understand and often find, even if it is surrounded by red, orange, yellow, green, blue, and purple. We need to take PRIDE in every type of love. I am proud that my oldest has taught me how to think more broadly about sex, gender, and love.

LLL Number 8

HAPPILY EVER LAUGHTER

Love loves to love love.
—James Joyce

If I picture my happiest moments, they are pretty subtle. Will holding my hand while walking down the beach or lying on the sofa with Will and Felix watching *House Hunters International*. When I picture my joyous moments, though, those are the ones when I am laughing in such an intense way that I am crying or feeling as if I am about to pee in my pants. You know that laughter when you just cannot stop. The kind when it is impossible to feel any kind of sad because your giggles are so deep they penetrate your entire being. Both Will and my youngest, as well as my oldest bonus child, can make me laugh like that.

Life is hard and stressful. There seems to be a baseline intensity to every single day since the pandemic; it could bring you down if you focus on it all the time. So you have to laugh. Sure, you can count on all those comedians out there. I rarely miss a laugh when I am scrolling Instagram and Nate Bargatze pops up or when my youngest and I are sitting and watching *Curb Your Enthusiasm*, a John Mulaney special, or listening to a *SmartLess* podcast together. But the only way to integrate laughter into your daily life is to find someone who can make you laugh.

I am not suggesting dating a stand-up comedian, but everyone has a different sense of humor. I learned this fact by watching my parents. My dad, God bless him, says the silliest things that make my mom laugh out loud. I cannot count the number of times that my dad has cracked (sorry, Dad) the dumbest joke at a table filled with people, and my mom is literally the only one laughing. Isn't that the epitome of love?

From probably date number two, Will has shared his witty, fairly dry sense of humor that always makes me laugh. Sometimes he gets on a roll, and I truly feel as if I will die laughing. I am not sure many people would think that Will's comic bantering is "to die for" funny, but they are my lifeblood. Take Will on vacation, give him a cocktail and an ocean view, and he actually is a stand-up comedian. I think I can make him laugh as well, although I am losing it a bit as I age. A good goal for me to work on in retirement.

While Will can be intense as well, it's during the times when I seem to need it the most that he makes me laugh. I remember being so incredibly nervous when we went to his various appointments during the cancer process. He must have been a mess inside, but instead of showing it, he made these silly jokes about pink being his new favorite color and the fact that he was going to get his other man boob removed too so he can finally look like a Ken doll. Maybe these jokes seem in bad taste or over-the-top, but at the time, they allowed us to both lighten our hearts and our minds.

Please do not minimize the need for silly and witty in your lives, and I don't mean just sending each other reels on Instagram. Make sure you can share laughter as well as tears with your person. It will make your life so much more enjoyable. Just remember that funny to you is what matters, and it does really matter.

LLL Number 9

HEARTS DON'T TAKE ORDERS

True love cannot be found where it does not exist,
nor can be denied where it does.
—Torquato Tasso

If I had a dollar for every time someone told me, "Just try a second date. You never know; you may end up liking him," or "You need to be more open-minded and go out again," well then, I would be retired and living on the ocean in California. It was a very long nine and a half years of trying to find the one. I will admit that there were a few times that I did go on a second date because on paper the person seemed so fabulous, but at the end of the day, there was just no connection. I really do believe in chemistry.

I believe in it for love of all kinds, including friendships. Some people have chemistry, and some do not. If you do not have chemistry with someone, I believe that you cannot generate it out of thin air. And I don't mean just sexual chemistry; although, that is fabulous too.

While my data gathering and personal experiences taught me that you need to have an open heart and an open mind to meet someone, you cannot and should not force it. I happen to be the kind of person who tends to decide on someone within the first fifteen minutes of meeting them. I will admit that I have been wrong on occasion—virtually never about guys I was dating, but about potential friends and even colleagues. And I mean wrong in both directions, for the good and the bad. Some people just take longer to get to know and may originally be nervous or anxious or introverted or may seem amazing, but instead are just excellent at faking it.

The reason I think that the judgment is different with love is because either you feel the chemistry or you do not. I am a huge fan of a second date if there is any possibility of that connection because first dates have to be the most awkward thing ever. Will and I love sitting at a restaurant and trying to figure out who is on their first date. This silly exercise also allows me to thank my lucky stars that I am sitting with Will and not at the table across the way, attempting to be interested in someone talking about what he lifted at the gym or how far he ran.

I was always enamored with shows that focused on arranged marriages, although I recognize that this could be potentially contradictory to this LLL. I have not missed an episode of *Indian Matchmaker* or *Jewish Matchmaker*. I am always rooting for true love to happen, but based on my recent Google searches, none of the matches from these shows are still together. It is TV, after all. Yet maybe these matchmakers can see the chemistry and potential connection that we cannot see ourselves.

My only real attempt at using a matchmaker was the Lunch Date service I mentioned earlier, which was a very pricey dating service I decided to purchase about a year before I met Will. Back when I participated, it started with an in-person meeting and a live analysis by a proposed "expert" matchmaker, rather than just filling out some random online dating profile. Keep in mind, though, that Lunch Date's whole menu included only those professional guys who also were desperate enough to pay a ridiculous fee to be set up on a lunch date with someone they would not see a picture of in advance, thus making this service much different than online dating. The starting premise was that everyone was a "professional," but otherwise, to participate, you had to agree to go to lunch with whomever this so-called expert selected for you. As I shared earlier, my first two lunch dates were so bad I demanded a refund. Apparently, there was a no-returns policy though, so I just considered the money a donation for others to find love. Needless to say, this "expert" matchmaker did not find a connection for me. So this LLL is just my advice to not force it. There really does need to be an ease to the process. Sure, there may be challenges, like kids or long distances or exes, but the connection itself needs to be easy peasy, lemon squeezy, not stressy depressy, lemon zesty. If it is too difficult, it is not meant to be, and as amazing as someone seems, they may not be your someone.

LLL Number 10

DON'T HAVE TOO MANY RULES

Fortune and love favor the brave.
—Ovid

When I first decided to put myself on the dating market, I literally wrote down a list of rules. As a die-hard rule follower, I decided that these guideposts would allow me to stay focused and not repeat any bad decisions. And to be fair to me, when all the people around me constantly asked me what I was looking for, I needed to be able to explain my criteria in order for a fix-up to have any potential. What I learned through this process is that you need to have standards, but not dating rules.

My first rule was age. Initially, I was good with a potential match no more than five years older or younger. Interestingly, I ended up dating someone almost ten years younger than I was, as I explained earlier, and it did not work, but it was my best relationship other than Will. Plus, age is so arbitrary. Fifty on me may be different than fifty on you. The focus should be on likes, dislikes, and outlooks. While Will and I are nine and a half years apart, I never feel it. He keeps up with me. (Ha, I have to keep up with him!) We work out together with a trainer, we walk for hours together when we travel, and yes, the sex is as if we were teenagers. He may nap more often than I, but I am not sure his love of naps is an age thing.

There are times when he brings up a show or a song or a movie, and then he realizes I was not born yet or maybe I was in kindergarten, but that always gives us a good laugh. We surround ourselves with people younger than we are, my age, his age, and even older—this wide net of friends allows us to learn and grow, and any age difference between us disappears. What I am saying is that it makes good sense to have an open mind and to focus on the person, not the number. Will's extra life experience brings so much wisdom to the table, and we have four kids to remind us how old we both are and what we have both been through.

The other big rule I had was that any potential suitor had to be fully divorced for at least a year. My initial rationale was that most guys need to have some fun when they break free from a marriage, and they do not want to immediately settle down. I did not want to be somebody's rebound. Plus, I had no stomach for a messy divorce or drama. Honestly, giving up this rule to go out with Will at the time was a tough one for me. Will was already well into the divorce process, but it took some time, so he was not quite officially divorced yet. The more potentially problematic fact in my mind was that he had not been on a single date in twenty-seven years, since he met his ex-wife.

Good old matchmaker Ann can be persuasive though, and I quickly realized what was important was that Will had moved on from his past and was focused on his future. That lens to the future was critical, not whether the paperwork had been signed just yet. If the person you are dating is totally honest with you about where they are and where they are going, then that honesty is a foundation on which to build something special. If there are some hurdles to get over, they may be worth jumping for the right person.

I won't even mention my rules about looks, as that is really individual. I probably could not date someone six foot five if I ever wanted to kiss him, and as I just explained, I was turned off by my lunch date who was literally shorter than I. This is a physical attraction thing for which there can be no rules.

The only rule I would still endorse is that I wanted someone who was a professional in the way I was, as I needed someone to understand my work life, which included my professional expectations and goals. Although I ideally did not want to date a lawyer, I still dated a few and remained open-minded on whether a JD was a fit for me. If you want a lively discussion, putting a defense lawyer and a plaintiff's lawyer in a bar together on a first date produces some interesting content. I recall a very heated debate about damage limits or something to that effect that did not bode well for our future. There was no second date.

Will and I are lucky to have so much in common from a work perspective that it allows us to support each other in ways I never imagined. As an environmental lawyer, I work with some niche statutes and regulations that Will weirdly knows and understands from his world. The overlap can be scary, and we tend to be each other's best sounding board for both projects and challenges. I explain this just to say that the need for a professional who understood my world was essential to me because I knew it would be an important component of the success of our relationship.

This rule certainly may not be applicable to everyone. I can imagine, for example, that a dedicated artist may ideally want a partner who is a creative type so she can appreciate his commitment to his passion. Additionally, at least one of my love stories was a couple who were both doctors. They both confirmed that the understanding that comes with sharing the same overall profession truly helped their marriage. I can only imagine their dinner-table conversations.

Overall, this rule follower is so glad she abandoned some of those silly initial parameters, as they just hold you back from potentially meeting your happily ever after. I suggest revisiting any limitations to see if they really make sense for you, and perhaps opening yourself up to something beyond your original framework to make that dream of love a reality.

The Final LLL

DO NOT SETTLE

*Love is born into every human being; it calls back the
halves of our original nature together; it tries to make
one out of two and heal the wound of human nature.*

—Plato

My wish is that if only one phrase from of all my love and
dating sagas sticks with you, it is **"Please do not settle."**
My children have heard me say this countless times, more
so recently as they continue to go through their twenties
and start to consider what their adult lives and loves
might include. I have talked to so many people who feel
ready to be married but cannot find the one. Instead of
waiting, I have watched those folks pick what appears to
be the best of the bunch at the time and make it work. They
may not be listening to their gut, or they may just feel that
they may not ever find anyone who will be a better fit for
their life.

I hope to be able to look at each of my kids' future partners and be thrilled that they found their equal, someone who will make them a better person, support them through all life's challenges, and let them share their darkest secrets and deepest fears. It's what I wanted for so long and what I saw that others seemed to have with so much more ease and less drama. My childhood bestie told me several times years ago that everything seems to be a bit more difficult for me, but it does seem to work out in the end. Well, that is the truth, and I embrace a good challenge.

For whatever reason, we tend to get restless or maybe we feel we are in too deep. I can assure you that unraveling a relationship that is not the right one for you long term, before marriage, will be much easier than unraveling it two kids, two houses, and many years later. I always admired my ex-brother-in-law when he broke off an engagement a while back that was not right for him. They were living together at the time—the whole kit and caboodle. He is now married to a real gem; they are a perfect fit and have the cutest two boys. I think about his courage and hope that others can emulate it and be strong enough to walk away when something is not right, rather than stay because it's easier.

The inability to challenge yourself, to have enough self-confidence, or to think of yourself as worthy of true love leads to regretful decisions that can impact where your life goes and how windy and bumpy that path may be along the way. Plus, we are talking about trying to figure out a foggy and challenging area. It's so important to do this hard work so that you can spot the one when that person comes along, rather than be stuck in a relationship that is not working.

The visual I would give you is of two people with two separate minds, but one shared heart. This visual arises from a piece of art in our home. Will and I went to Cabo on our honeymoon. We loved to travel at the time and, in fact, planned the honeymoon before we finalized our wedding plans. During the trip, we ventured to a cool art walk in San Jose del Cabo, where we found and later purchased a painting titled *Two Minds, One Heart* by Sosa. It is a large, quintessentially modern piece of art with an outline of a man's head on the left and a women's head on the right, but in the middle, there is one red circle with lots of lines representing the connectedness of the couple. We love art and are lucky to have some wonderful pieces, but our honeymoon purchase remains my favorite work. It is truly the visual of what I had achieved and what I want for each and every one of our kids. We have kept our independent selves, but we now walk around with a piece of each other's heart, joined as one because we did not settle.

CONCLUSION

To love and be loved is the most
natural expression of our being.
—Deepak Chopra

I have been interested in the concept of love for much of my life. I grew up watching my parents who demonstrated the model love story. There were lots of "I love yous" floating around my house. Yet, somehow and in some way, I did not feel worthy. I worked hard to address that feeling, as well as to understand what love looks and feels like for many people. It is comforting to know that love really is subjective, but yet there are common foundational pieces that can be assessed as you are searching for your person.

I did not understand this concept back when my journey started. In my first postdivorce journal entry, dated September 11, 2008, I wrote:

> *I cannot help but contemplate how life got so*
> *complicated and difficult. I am truly at a loss of*

energy —whatever that means. I am not sure how I keep up as a mom, lawyer, friend, daughter. I have so many wonderful people in my life, but I am so lonely. How is that? Will I ever be free of all this pain, or am I destined to a life of misery, never able to truly break free. I have made so many bad choices, and I feel as if I continue to make them. I must break this cycle. I have to find happiness in myself and then others, most importantly my kids. I cannot go on carrying this burden and all this pain. It is too much to bear, and it is blocking my ability to break free and start my new life.

What transpired in the five years between when I wrote that entry and when I met Will is nothing short of a miracle. I grew so much as a person and as a mother. I learned so many new things about myself and about the importance of love. I learned about what long-term, solid relationships look and feel like and that love stories can have challenges but also so much joy. I learned that embracing the uncertainty and taking a few risks can lead to so much happiness.

It is perhaps ironic that as part of our wedding, we very much wanted the kids to know that our new love would in no way change our love for each of them. As I have said several times, you can never have enough people who love you. Thus, as an Indiana guy, Will and I decided to gift each of the four kids a small Robert Indiana *Love* sculpture as a reminder that they are loved, and they will continue to be loved. I look at that sculpture now with the *L* and *O* stacked on the *V* and *E* and appreciate the symbolism of individuals in love connected in a way that creates balance and beauty. It was the perfect representation of what we both felt and wanted to share with our family when we finally came together.

It is this love that I know will carry us through our future challenges and our happiest days. It's a love I never thought I would be privileged enough to receive or to give. It's a feeling that is so hard to describe, but yet so clear and so grounding. I am so grateful that my journey (albeit bumpy and winding) led me to my own love story that I can share with you.

ACKNOWLEDGMENTS

I would not have a story to share if it were not for my dear Will. I have already explained my gratefulness that he is my true partner, but I also am thankful that he was brave enough and open enough to allow me to share our love story.

Thank you to Morgan and Zach, who survived the 104 dates without knowing that I was even dating (I hope) and who sometimes saw me when I was less than my best self as they were growing up. Your love was then and still remains my foundation, and I carry your hearts in mine.

Thank you to Max and Ben, who were likely less than pleased when they had to deal with another "mom" in their life. They are one of my greatest gifts, just like their dad, and I am grateful for their support and for allowing me to become part of their lives.

There are no words to thank Ann Zoller for bringing Will into my life. Her wisdom, intuition, and kindness parallel no one I have ever met. She was then and remains part of our family, a dear friend, and my fairy godmother. I also have to thank Tami Schneider for founding Cleveland

Yoga and creating a place for me to meet Ann and my Front Row Crew that led me to Will. Tami's friendship and the community she created changed my life in so many ways.

Thank you to Claudia, who pops up throughout the book. Claudia was basically my life partner after I was separated and then divorced, as I tried my best to continue to raise my kids with love without neglecting myself. While she initially joined us as an au pair, she eventually became family. I would have never been able to date or follow the journey that led me to Will if she were not an unwavering part of my children's life and a rock for me.

Thank you to Nana and Patti, who like Claudia helped me survive my single-mom days, working and dating. While Nana has left this earth, she is a cornerstone of my research project and one of my life heroes. Auntie Patti, as my kids know her, also never said no to watching the kids, sleepovers, or just helping when I needed it for a break or maybe a date.

There are no words as well to thank my parents for the example they set for me about true love and for the unconditional love they have provided to me and my kids throughout some challenging times.

My village is my everything. I thank so many of them for participating in my interviews back in 2009–2010 and for those in my newly expanded village who participated in my most recent interviews. I am not going to name names so that the research remains private, but I will say that if it were not for my dear friends, near and far, not only would my life be much less fun, I truly do not think I would have survived or at least remained sane, which

I know might be debatable. There were physical helping hands when I needed it, honest conversations, invites to dinners, food drop-offs (especially when Will had cancer), phone calls, and just lots of love. Each of you know who you are, and I hope you know that you are my family.

Thank you to Heather Ettinger, who encouraged me to continue writing my book and to publish it so that I can share my story with others. She remains a true role model and guiding light.

I have to thank Cheryle Gainer and my work family even though this book is not about work. Cheryle is probably the main reason I have been able to maintain a successful career and be efficient enough to date and now to write a book while making sure my client relationships remain a priority. My work family (you know who you are) has given me the support I needed personally and professionally for the journey I have been on over the past few decades.

Finally, I thank Halo Publishing for all of the guidance they provided during my adventure in becoming an author. I am grateful to be able to tell my story with the hopes that it may lead others to find true love.

MEET THE AUTHOR

Heidi B. Friedman, formerly Goldstein and born Eisman, is a successful attorney and partner at a large law firm specializing in all areas of environmental law and environmental, social, and governance-based counseling (ESG). *Love Lessons* is her first book, but Heidi has written regularly for *Bloomberg, Law 360,* and other publications related to her professional life and experience as a female lawyer.

Heidi lives in Cleveland Heights, Ohio, with her husband, Will, and their joint baby, Felix, a cur mix they rescued. Will is Heidi's do-over after being single for almost ten years and surviving 104 dates.

Heidi has four children. Two children she birthed, Morgan (25) and Zach (21), and two are her bonus children, Max (28) and Ben (26).

Heidi and Will greatly enjoy traveling as well as spending time with friends. Heidi likes walks around Shaker Lakes, her time at yoga and Pilates, and date nights at a bar with Will. In her life, she has a strong network of amazing women whom she treasures and who provide support, guidance, and company for drinking wine.

LET'S CONNECT

Find out more about Heidi B. Friedman
at the following links!

Email: lovelessons104@gmail.com

Instagram: @lovelessons104

Facebook: Love Lessons: 104 Dates
and the Stories that Led Me to True Love

LinkedIn: Heidi B. (Goldstein) Friedman